GW00400286

Thin Black Lines

- political cartoons & development education

written and compiled by

Colm Regan, Scott Sinclair, Martyn Turner.

Published by and available from:

Development Education Centre,
Selly Oak Colleges, Bristol Road,
Birmingham, B29 6LE.

© **Development Education Centre, 1988.**

ISBN: 0 - 948838 - 02 - 7

Introduction

Political cartoons have a lot to say about the state of the world. Their role in the media is significant but their use as a stimulus to learning has been limited. **'Thin Black Lines'** sets out to encourage people involved in education, whether in schools or with informal adult groups, to exploit the potential of political cartoons for stimulating greater awareness of world issues.

It is a cliche to say that the world is getting smaller but it is nevertheless true. It is also arguably becoming more complex, more unequal, more unjust and ultimately, in a nuclear age, more unstable. We need to understand this for it affects us all. Development Education is about these issues. It is about how the world relates to us and how we relate to the world.

'Thin Black Lines' is published by the Development Education Centre, Birmingham which is an educational charity. The three authors discovered by accident their common interest in the potential of cartoons in education.

The three of us: Colm Regan [Head of Education Department, Trocaire]; Martyn Turner [political cartoonist with The Irish Times] and Scott Sinclair [Co-ordinator of the Development Education Centre] have put this book together when other work brought us into the same proximity. The book is a by-product of co-operation over work on more long term curriculum development projects.

The main sections of the book are made up of collections of cartoons arranged around themes or issues. We have also set out to include a wide range of cartoon styles. Each section begins with a lead article which introduces the main issues. In addition to the activities in the introduction there are suggestions for using the cartoons in each section. There is also other information which can be used in group discussion. Clearly there are many combinations of cartoons which could be used in different ways according to the work in hand. The activities outlined can also be easily adapted for use with other cartoons.

We are not claiming that using cartoons should be given any special place as a teaching method but that they should be taken more seriously as a stimulus for tackling complex issues. However if we are to use cartoons in learning then there is a need to build up skills in "reading" cartoons in order that they can be used to their full potential.

Contents

Using political cartoons in development education

Political cartoons can be a particularly valuable resource for development education. They, at their best, encapsulate some very complex issues, different viewpoints and some of the contradictions which are a real part of many situations. Political cartoons do not simply take sides, they offer a challenge to us all. They can make links between issues which sometimes turn them inside out. They don't spare our sensitivities - this is their essential strength.

Political cartoons will often provide the stimulus to stop and think, to look sideways or look afresh at a particular issue. We hope that readers of this book will find much to provide a focus for personal reflection. However the main purpose of this introductory section is to outline a few basic activities for the use of cartoons in group discussion.

A word of warning may be useful here. If you see education in general, or development education in particular, as a process of endorsing certain "acceptable" ideas or viewpoints and rejecting others, rather than as a means of exploring, discussing and debating ideas and opinions as a means of encouraging people to make up their own minds, then don't use cartoons. It is unlikely that they will provide enough opportunity for control!

Cartoons have a number of advantages as a stimulus to group discussion about issues. They often contain a lot of information yet can be assimilated quite quickly. It is possible for people with a range of knowledge of the issues [or none at all] to respond to the same stimulus and for the discussion to reflect their level of experience. The humour of cartoons also contributes to the groups interactions, laughter is important but this humour can also dissarm us of our assumptions and help us look afresh at the issues. Many of the cartoons you might choose to use as a stimulus will be quite explicit in the main issues they bring to the group's agenda, they are however at the same time very open ended. They provide the opportunity for a group to explore the aspects they see as most important or most at issue.

WHO ?

J. F. Batellier   France

JF.Batellier.
2/97

The activities outlined here and in each of the main sections of the book can be adapted to a wide range of learning situations. It is however important to note that we need to build up our skills in group discussion and in using stimulus material such as cartoons.

The learning skills that can be developed by using material such as cartoons include:

- making careful observations

- acquiring information from the cartoon

- analysing and evaluating information

- relating one's own views to those in the cartoons

- recognising the value of different interpretations

- empathising with the people / situations portrayed

- forming links between the ideas in different cartoons

There is a sense in which cartoons can help us to laugh at ourselves and our involvement, individually and as a society, in fairly desperate situations. Perhaps we should identify this as a skill too.

'Thin Black Lines' has five main sections. Each begins with a lead cartoon and a short introduction to the issues. In addition to the collections of cartoons there are also some other short pieces of text which could be used as part of the stimulus material for group work. These are linked together by some brief suggestions on how these could be used. Each section ends with some suggested background reading and other useful material.

The following are some ideas which could provide the framework for planning to use any cartoons. In particular there are some suggestions for introducing them in a group.

Warming up - What does it say to you?

You could ask this question of any cartoon but there is special value in asking it about one which is open to very wide interpretation such as those on pages 4 -7.

The discussion moves quite rapidly away from the cartoon to the interests and concerns of the members of the group. This kind of activity is particularly valuable when you are trying to work with a new group, or when people in the group don't know each other very well. A reasonable amount of time should be allowed for people to work on their initial thoughts and to share ideas.

A closer look - Now you see it now you don't

There are a number of simple activities which encourage students to take a closer look at the cartoon and to articulate how they see it.

For example... Working in pairs each has their own cartoon. They look at the cartoon without showing it to their partner. Then turn over the cartoons and describe to each other what they are about. Then compare these descriptions with the cartoons. What was left out? How is the cartoon different from how you imagined it from your partner's description?

Reading a cartoon....

At an early stage it may be useful to take time out to discuss one or two cartoons and work on "reading" them.

Ask small groups to look closely at the details

- what is the cartoon saying?
- what different interpretations do they imagine could be made?
- what symbols are used?
- who are the characters?
- what is suggested about the context of the cartoon?

Bring the groups together to share their discussion but steer the discussion away from any issues that arise and concentrate on how they read the cartoons.

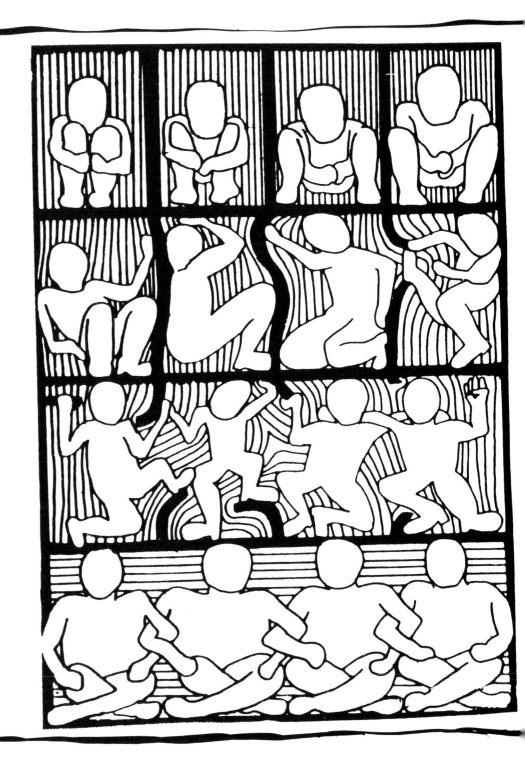

Plantu France

What's the theme? - What are the issues?

When you introduce a theme to a group it is useful to find ways to explore what the group already knows about it and how best to build on this in order to work on the issues in more depth.

Display a collection of cartoons [say 15-20] and ask the group to look at them. Working in pairs decide what main theme[s] link them as a collection. They could then choose a number of cartoons [say 3-5] which highlight the main issues as they see them and arrange them into a poster which they share with the rest of the group.

Sharing views

Another useful way to introduce a collection of cartoons is to ask people to choose three cartoons from those on display which they like most .... or which say most to them about the issues being considered. They could mark these with a sticker with their name on. They could then pair up with someone who has chosen the same cartoons and discuss their choice. Are the reasons the same? Did they see different things in the same cartoon?

This activity also has the advantage of mixing the group, reviewing the whole collection and working at some cartoons more closely. The pairs can then share the highlights of their discussion and introduce one of the cartoons they chose to the rest of the group.

Headlining .... changing the context

Ask pairs to choose a cartoon around which they develop a headline and/or short article. If they use different headlines does it influence how the cartoon comes over?

The pairs could then share their article with the rest of the group. It may be useful to choose different cartoons and therefore raise a wide range of issues or choose the same one and explore the different ways it is worked into the article.

You could also use a cartoon like the one on this page. The original cartoon said Luxembourg, Bruxelles and Strasbourg on the sign posts ... what would your group wish to put on them? You could then review some of the detail, the ten men and ten stars for example.

Questioning and asking questions

It is valuable both as an introductory activity or when you are wanting to discuss more detailed issues to focus on one or two cartoons and make a more detailed study of them.

Give each pair a copy of a cartoon mounted on a large sheet of paper and ask them to write as many questions as they can relating to the cartoon. This encourages a closer look at detail as well as the cartoon as a whole. It is not necessary to be able to answer the questions, the process of asking them will provide a good stimulus to the discussion when they share their work with other groups.

Another approach which would help more detailed study of one cartoon is for you to pose the questions for the group to consider. In order to encourage a group to discuss the cartoon opposite, for example, you could ask questions such as the following:

- What does the cartoon suggest about the relationship between the USA and the USSR?
- What does it suggest about the relationship between the interests of the two super-powers and those of the "Third World"?
- What image do you have of the USA and the USSR?
- Do you tend to think of similarities between them or differences?
- How do they talk to each other?
- Why is the "Third World" not represented by a political figure?
- Does it suggest anything to you about the relationship between different "Third World" countries?

Martyn Turner Ireland

Ranking

This is a very effective activity to encourage groups to consider a small collection of cartoons [say nine] in detail. Give each group nine cartoons and ask them to order them in terms of those they feel raise the most important issues - to those that raise the least important. Alternatively you could ask pairs to rank the cartoons in terms of those they like most/ least.

Suggest that they rank them in a diamond pattern such as the one here. When they have done this they can compare their ranking with those of other groups. This can lead to a full discussion because the task makes sure everyone has been involved in thinking about the issues.

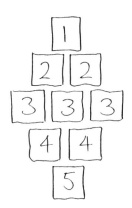

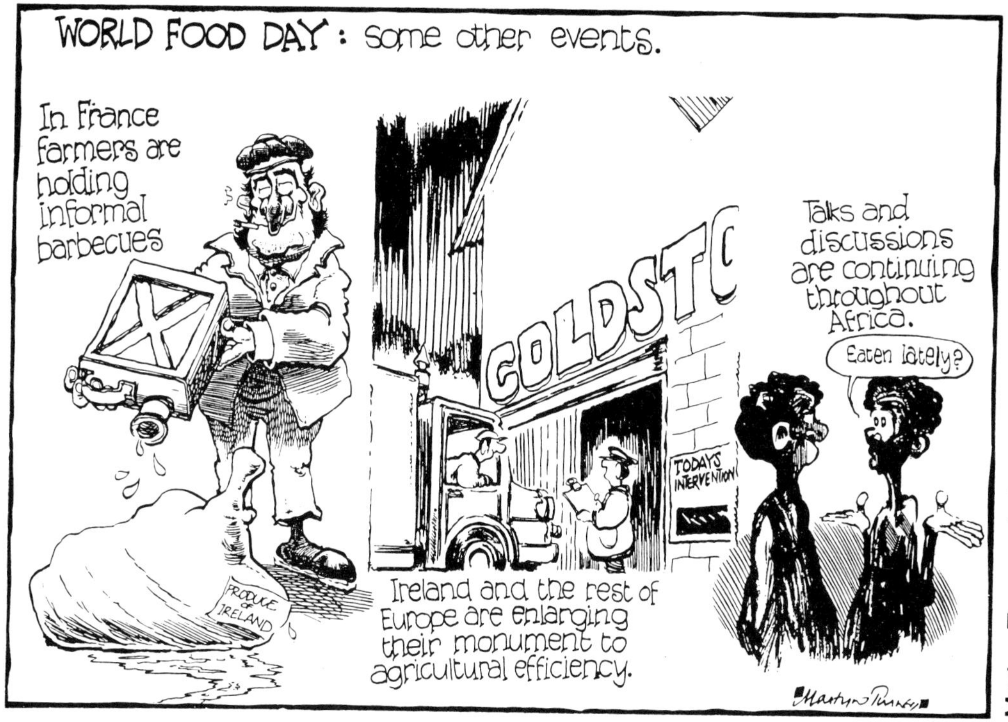

WORLD FOOD DAY : Some other events.
In France farmers are holding informal barbecues
PRODUCE OF IRELAND
COLDSTO
TODAYS INTERVENTION
Ireland and the rest of Europe are enlarging their monument to agricultural efficiency.
Talks and discussions are continuing throughout Africa.
Eaten lately?

Martyn Turner Ireland

Naji al Ali Lebanon

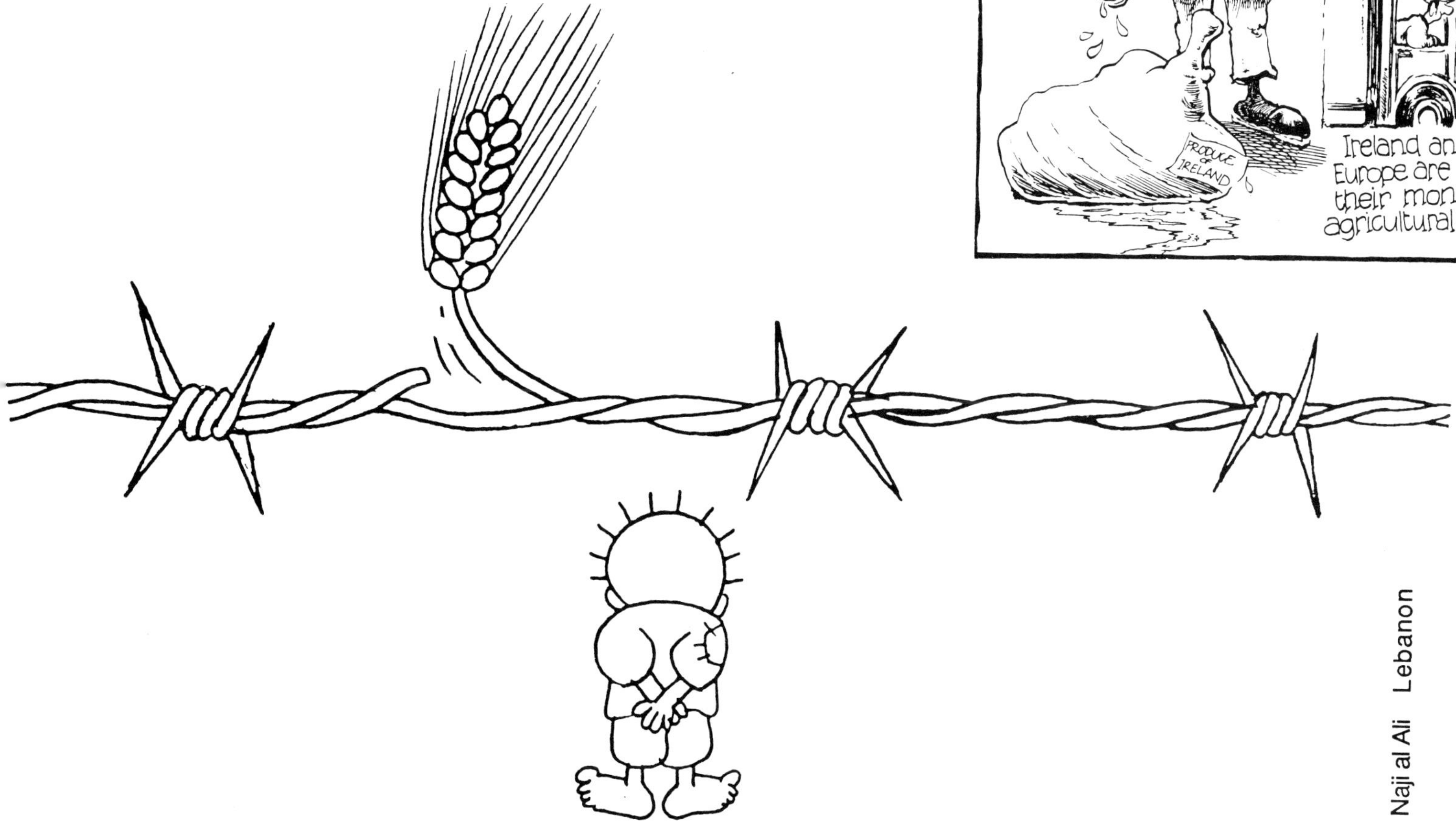

A history of political cartoons

Some books would have us believe that political cartooning and caricaturing first appeared on earth some time during the late 16th century. Evolution apparently took that long to produce a creature that could combine art, portraiture and political comment in the same picture. But this dating would leave out the Ancient Greek who drew his opinion of the local Queen on the wall of a cave. Subsequently, and rapidly, he became an artist in exile when his adoring audience turned out to be part of the Queen's army (a loyal part).

In 1590 Annibale and Agostini Carracci, brothers and Italian at the same time, produced a series of drawings called ritratini carichi (loaded portraits) from which evolved the term "caricature". For the next hundred years caricaturing flourished on the Continent from which the art took another leap forward with the mutations of William Hogarth in England. Hogarth's contribution was to widen the scope of caricaturing and to create a whole series of drawings which commented on the social issues of the times. In 1734 he published "A Harlot's Progress" which was followed by "A Rake's Progress" in 1735 and "Marriage A La Mode" in 1745.

'Join or Die' Cartoon by Ben Franklin. 1754

Meanwhile, in America Benjamin Franklin, Statesman, inventor and kite flier, extended the function of the cartoon to include propaganda. His simple but effective cartoon titled "Join or Die" appeared in the Pennsylvanian Gazette in 1754.

The successors to Hogarth in England were Thomas Rowlandson and James Gillray; the former specialising in social issues, the latter in politics - especially England's relationship with France during the Revolution and the Napoleonic Wars.

Meanwhile ....Francisco Goya is probably best known as a portrait painter and as the artist who produced the "Maja" in both clothed and unclothed version. But Goya was essentially a satirist and a commentator on contemporary Spain. During a lull in the censorship laws he published a series of drawings entitled "Los Caprichos" in 1797.

Such titles as: - "He broke a jug." - "Will the pupil be any wiser?" - "May God forgive her"; and "It was her mother!" give an idea of the range of the contents of the satire.

In 1810, following Napoleon's invasion of Spain, Goya produced a further series of engravings called "Disasters of War". His need to caricature to express his feelings extended beyond his engravings into his official work. His portraits of the Spanish Royal family have been described by one biographer as a "highly critical if not savagely satirical view of a royal house which we know to have been weak, foolish and decadent".

Later in the 19th century the Royal Family of France became the staple diet of the caricaturist Honore Daumier. So successful was Daumier at his trade that he earned the supreme accolade in 1831 - he was imprisoned by King Louis Philippe. His cartoon entitle "gargantua" showing KLP as a bloated monster was worth six months in the pokey. In 1834 he achieved the wrath of the entire French legislature with ~"The Legislative Belly" which showed the politicians as one huge stomach eating up the wealth of the nation.

Francisco Goya's Disaster 61. **'Are they of another race?'**

11

His reward for this one was a new censorship law which caused Daumier to move away from directly political themes to more general attacks on the system. He achieved even greater success with a series of drawings with such titles as "Solid Citizenz", "Matrimonial Mores" and "Philanthropists of the Day". He turned then to painting, reviving his cartoons to attack Napoleon and to support the Paris Commune in 1871. He died in obscurity in 1879. After death, like Buddy Holly, he became famous.

The career of Daumier is in many ways reflected in the life of America's father of cartooning, Thomas Nast. Nast was described during the American Civil War by Abraham Lincoln as the Northern States "best recruiting sergeant" following the appearance of his cartoons in Harpers Weekly. But in 1870 Nast achieved a degree of power and influence which has probably been unequalled by any cartoonist since. His savage drawings depicting the corrupt New York political group known as the Tweed Ring led eventually to the entire group being either voted out of office or taken to court. At one stage attempts were made to bribe Nast into silence. The sum offered started small and rose eventually to half a million dollars but (foolishly!) he kept on drawing and introduced "Tammany Hall" into the language as a simile for corruption and saw the Mayor, William Marcy Tweed, flee the country. Such is the transient nature of good political cartooning that, despite many university and school courses based on the Tammany Hall cartoons of Thomas Nast, he is probably best remembered as the artist who created the universally known image of Father Christmas.

Nast's work laid the guidelines for what is now known as political cartooning (or in the United States, editorial cartooning). Changes in this century have been mainly changes in style. The detailed work of engravings and wood blocks gave way to a simplified style made famous by David Low in the UK and then to the free flowing, more surreal style of today. This was made possible by the acceptance of the work of Ronald Searle in the 1950's and 60's.,-[the influence, stylistically on almost every political cartoonist working today]. This impressionist style was carried on by Ralph Steadman, Gerald Scarfe in Britain and Jeff MacNelly and Pat Oliphant in the United States.

The upsurge in political cartooning in America in recent years has been attributed to Richard Nixon. When he came into office there were about one hundred full time editorial cartoonists in the States. At the end of "Watergate" there were over two hundred!

In 1902 Thomas Wanamaker, owner of the Philadelphia North American and would be politician, charged his cartoonists with the task of destroying local Republican Senator, Matthew S. Quay and his appointee Samuel Pennypacker, in the belief that Quay stood between him and his political ambitions.

The cartoonists, Charles Nelan and Walt McDougall, both highly paid importees from New York, set about their task and throughout the years 1902 and 1903 proved to be both successes and failures. They failed inasmuch as their main target, Samuel Pennypacker, was elected with a 140,000 majority much of which came from within the circulation area of the Philadelphia North American. They succeeded, on the other hand, to so upset the political powers with their cartoons and caricatures that the State Legislature passed an "Anti Cartoon Law". It made it a crime "to draw or publish any cartoon or caricature or picture portraying, describing, or representing any person either by distortion, innuendo, or otherwise, in the form or likeness of a beast, bird, fish, insect, or other inhuman animal". The fine applicable was 1,000 dollars or two years in jail.

McDougall's response is shown here on page 13.

There were a few prosecutions under the Act, none successful, and in 1907 one of the first things the new Governor and Legislature did was to repeal the law.

Cartoonists in context

On the next few pages we introduce the work and thoughts of three cartoonists. One from Eastern Europe, Jo Szabo who was the editor of Magyar Nemzet is now working in America. One from India, Suresh Sawant who works for The Times of India. Finally from Ireland, working with The Irish Times, Martyn Turner reflects on cartooning in the West.

McDOUGALL SHOWS PUSEY THE FATAL WEAKNESS OF HIS ANTI-CARTOON BILL AND HURLS DEFIANCE AT HIM

Because Assemblyman Pusey has introduced a bill in the Legislature, which aims to destroy the livelihood of a worthy, industrious and light-hearted class of mechanics, I feel called upon to defy him and to show that his efforts, by no matter whom they were originated, will avail him nothing. The bill forbids the use of "unhuman" animal forms in caricaturing human beings in this Commonwealth. So little appreciated are the diverse resources of a caricaturist and so restricted the scope of his genius is supposed to be by the legislator with the two-inch forehead and the six inch moustache area that he imagines he can shake off the gifted artist by closing the animal world to him. The cartoonist may be compelled to part with his zoo of trained performing parrots, owls, hens, bears, skunks and bats upon which he has hitherto depended for a poor living, but he will never give up his profession at the behest of a yap legislator.

Small as are the monetary rewards of the cartoonist, pitiful as is the mere stipend handed out to him every week, he still has a vast pride in his Art, and when one considers that it is perhaps, apart from officeholding, the only profession requiring no real toil and the only one in which brains are absolutely unnecessary, it will be easily seen why the cartoonist clings to his job.

Mr. Pusey's threat does not cause us to quail. After the bill is passed even that word quail will be prohibited, I suppose, but that is en passant, as we say in Atlantic City. No action has yet been taken by the Cartoonists' Union in opposing this bill, not because we are afraid to go to Harrisburg and face the Legislature, but because even if it passes we can still do business at the old stand in the same old way. I submit several drawings to show that the Pussycat's bill is fatally weak. He should have included more than the animal kingdom alone, for we have an ample field in the vegetable if not even the mineral kingdom. An untried field too, fuller perhaps of possibilities than the old biological branch.

Every cartoonist has a Noah's Ark full of worn, broken and decrepit animals, bugs and such, but the fresh vegetable field is untouched. What chances of caricature lie in the tomato, the string bean, the cucumber, the onion and the leek cannot be guessed. I have made a few studies showing the possibilities of the carrot, squash, potato and chestnut, just to show what a journeyman cartoonist can do when pushed to the wall. Mr. Scot can take warning by these.

He must understand, too, that these are snapshots, dashed off without much reflection or deep thought, and when the rest of the gang gets after the legislative feline he'll be bombarded clean off the fence.

One sample is submitted also to show what can be done with purely inanimate objects. There are many such beside the old Dutch stein which I have used that will adapt themselves to the purpose, but this will suffice to show Mr. Pusey what we can and will do if his silly bill passes. I suppose, however, that when he reads this Assemblyman Kitty will add the word "vegetable" to the bill and try to squelch us in that manner. But I still have several other deadly weapons in reserve, and I defy him to do his very kittenist.

Walt McDougall

Source: Richard Samuel West. "Target" August '86.

Joseph George Szabo

Political cartoons drawn by Eastern Europeans seem to be clearly distinguishable from those created by Western cartoonists. They radiate some kind of sadness and bitterness with each of their talking lines. They are hieroglyphs of the modern world. No titles, bubbles, captions are attached. Mutely outspoken, but strictly philosophical cartoons, never pointing at the government, any of its officials or at any of the problems and tragedies, that it is responsible for.

Are the Eastern Europeans cowards not to take a stand openly or is the "beating around the bush" way of commentary a necessity for survival? Definitely the latter. Like artists generally, the cartoonists are sensitive to problems. Problems, which occur everywhere regardless what form of government rules in that particular country. But where the system gets suspicious when a positive character on a drawing comes from the right side of the picture, there you have to exercise self-censorship in order to avoid attracting the attention of the authorities.

In most countries belonging to the Soviet Bloc, newspapers show their contempt for cartoons by where they place them in their pages. Editorials [reflecting the official party line rather than the view of the editor] always appear on the front page. Cartoons do not. Nor do they appear on the pages featuring international or domestic news. They intentionally denigrate the importance of the cartoon by placing it among miscellaneous newsclips in the back pages. Even if it is unthinkable to publish a cartoon about the Communist Party or its leaders, they want to play down the importance of cartoons in the role of forming society. For good measure, issues like religion, abortion, or minority rights are also taboo.

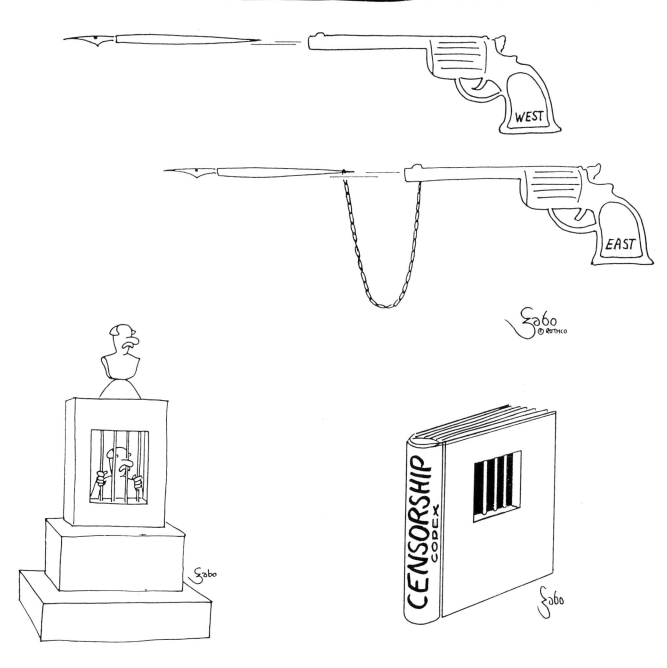

It is likely in the cartoonists' foraging that they might discover something hidden, a sensitive point, a purulent wound. They might point out a different way to go.

But this is what is unpardonable. "There is no better way than Communism". Anything different is considered opposition. If your cartoons are not in line with the Party, you are considered a potential enemy and as such you'll be eliminated from the pages of the publications. Since "the freedom of expression" is wisely included in the constitution, there is a simple and legitimate way to keep you away from the media. Although, you might be an award winner and once celebrated cartoonist, your cartoons suddenly will be produced in an "unprofessional manner".

So what can talented, benevolent cartoonists do, who love their vocation and want to take a positive part in the building of society, but are limited to cartoons corresponding to the party line? Since in a dictatorship it does not make sense to speak up openly, one has to be very witty and disciplined in order to stay on the safe side, but still be able to get a thoughtful message through.

The cartoonists want to be published, so they have to invent a harmless language for communication. The result is a sophisticated message wrapped into a more or less accepted form of art. These cartoons usually can be understood in more than one way [which is a protection for the artists], or their complicated message requires a very sophisticated mind to understand, so the bulk of these works is lost on the majority of people. Thus, only a very thin stratum of society can be effectively reached by these cartoons, which means that cartoon art as a form of visual communication is not able to play a substantial role in the development of Eastern European societies.

Suresh Sawant

written in collaboration with **Mohan Sivanand**

An interesting and politically important event took place in India in April this year. The editor of a popular Tamil* weekly from the southern state of India was arrested and put behind bars. [*Name of one of the major Indian languages]

His crime: publishing a cartoon which depicted local politicians as "thieves and pick-pockets". This joke, quite innocuous by Indian standards, enraged the members of the state's Legislative Assembly. The imprisonment of the editor, which could normally happen only under an autocratic government, shocked everyone here. The news instantly aroused anger and protest from every corner of the nation. Newspapers, particularly, screamed through strong-worded editorials -

   "Has democracy vanished from India?"
   "Is not the Press free here?"
   "Are our fundamental rights being crushed?"

The pressure from people and the Press was so strong, that ultimately the authorities had to release the editor unconditionally, within forty-eight hours of his arrest.

In any case, this was an isolated incident. India is a democratic country. Its Press is free. Indian cartoonists have every freedom to criticise anything. And Indians are always game for a joke. Yet, at the same time, one must always realise that India is basically a poor country striving to develop and industrialise. So, despite the unlimited freedom, cartoonists here aren't always as prosperous as their counterparts in developed Western nations.

So, here, even in a free democratic set up, we have instances of cartoonists toeing their bosses' line - especially since big business often has political

backing. [Or is it the other way round?].

Since Indian "cartoon syndicates" are still to take off, the foreign agencies such as King features Syndicate or Walt Disney's continue to do good business in this region. Indian comic books have made the scene relatively recently. Today, many are churned out by local publishers.

There are fourteen official languages in India and all of them have their publications. Yet, English is still wildly followed and gets importance as it used to get forty years ago, when India became independent of British rule. So, those who are associated with English journals are better known and even blindly followed by others. Cartoonists who draw for English newspapers are thus the 'leaders'.

A majority of Indian cartoonists consider their art a spare-time hobby. They have other 'more secure' occupations as their main source of income. They have to struggle hard to find time to draw or sell their cartoons. The encouragement is poor, and despite the poor quality of most cartoonists - the competition is fairly high.

A typical Indian cartoon is political. It's characters are politicians, identified by their 'Congress Caps' and Nehru jackets. The Indian politician - typically an elected member of Parliament or State Legislative Assembly - has the 'cartoon stereotype' of being talkative, stupid and crafty. With this background are the gags - on elections, public projects, political speeches and what-not. Social [not political] cartoning hasn't really come of age in India, and those who don't draw politics stay relegated to a few magazines. They rarely make it, however good they are, to the prestigious daily newspapers.

Martyn Turner

The first time I tried to write these words I started out by listing the hardships for European and American cartoonists and finished up convincing myself that there weren't any, assuming the brain and the hand keep going. But let me list a few of the hiccups.

1. Survival - The species, cartoonist politicos, tends to be as dependent as everyone else on a certain amount of income to feed, clothe and generally sustain himself. The fledgling cartoonist can expect at least ten years of foraging for scraps before he is able to sustain himself by his own efforts. Many fall by the wayside preferring the security of teaching, advertising or somesuch than trying to establish their cartooning credentials in a small publishing world.

2. Politics - Most political cartoonists are vaguely left wing. Most newspapers are vaguely right wing. This dilemma is resolved in different ways. A newspaper can agree to use a cartoonist for his nuisance value or as the devil's advocate of the editorial page. Thus the Evening Standard let David Low loose on its readership even allowing him to attack his own proprietor, Lord Beaverbrook, on a regular basis. Similarly Vicki, a life long Labour supporter, followed him in the same paper. Until 1986. Nicholas Garland managed to satisfy both the editors of the conservative Daily Telegraph and the socialist New Statesman with his work.

But some newspapers take a different approach. In a recent interview ("Target" Autumn 1986) the American cartoonist Dwane Powell describes his early (and only) days with the Cincinnati Enquirer.

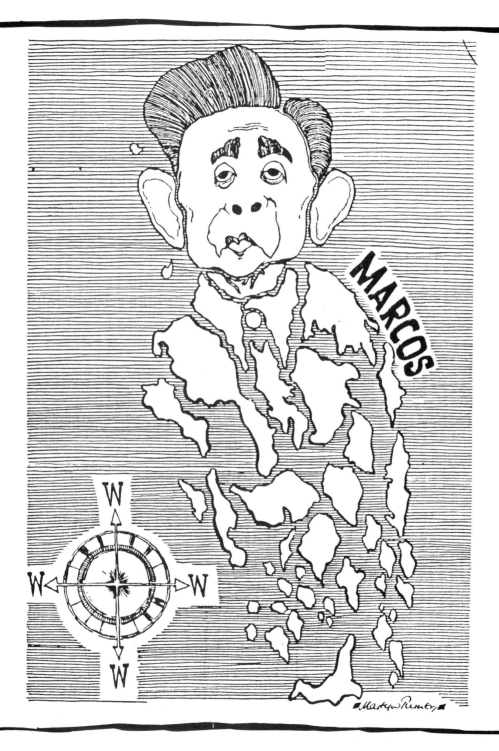

"The editorial page director came into my office one day and asked if I had been reading the Enquirer editorial pages. I said 'Yeah, I read them'. And he asked if I had noticed that my cartoons differed from their editorials. And I said yes but I reminded him that I showed him a rough every day...... Well, they gave me about three or four months to shape my act up........ I asked them if I had to read the editorials and draw cartoons saying essentially the same thing. And they said that was what a cartoonist was supposed to do. I told them I couldn't do that."
He now works for Raleigh News and Observer.

Some papers try to take a different approach. When Rupert Murdoch bought the Sunday Times he is alleged to have said, on seeing Scarfe's contribution in that week's paper [a drawing of the U.S. President], "Poor old Ronnie; we must get rid of this Pinko artist". Gerald Scarfe continues to express his own opinions in the Sunday Times.

3. Censorship . In Europe and America there is no legal censorship. An attempt in Canada to sue a cartoonist, successful in a lower court, caused panic among the artists, but was overturned on appeal and everyone lived happily ever after. Just before Christmas 1986 a journalist entering the United States at Newark Airport was turned away when it was discovered he had "socialist literature" in his baggage. No such restriction exists, however, on the inmates of the United States and a cartoon, if it gets past the editor, it usually gets past the law.

Cartooning, to quote Jeff MacNelly, "is a negative art. We rarely say anything nice in our cartoons." For the person prepared to spend his life being negative, to suffer a bit along the way, to forgo a pension, and to spend long hours wrestling with himself inside his own head, there are few restrictions to becoming a political cartoonist in "the West". Whatever their politics it is usually possible to find some publication to take on their work.

"I wish you wouldn't squeeze so", said the Dormouse, who was sitting next to her.

"I can hardly breathe".

"I can't help it", said Alice very meekly: "I'm growing".

"You've no right to grow here", said the Dormouse.

"Don't talk nonsense", said Alice more boldly:

"You know you're growing too".

"Yes, but I grow at a reasonable pace", said the Dormouse:

"Not in that ridiculous fashion"

[Lewis Carroll - Alice's Adventures in Wonderland]

Both the decades of the 1960's and 1970's were declared to be development decades by the United Nations. Particular attention was to be paid to policies and strategies which helped develop the poorest nations and, within them, the poorest people. The gap between the rich and poor was to be narrowed.

But if measured by income, the gap between the developed and Third World countries has widened over those decades. Incomes per head have risen in the First World from $1.407 to $6,468 a year while those of the Third World have increased from $132 to $579. Within most countries the gap between the richest and the poorest groups has also widened.

It therefore seems that current development increases social inequality rather than reduces it. The strategies put forward by the world's development "experts" seem to benefit a small minority disproportionately while disadvantaging the majority.

Traditionally the term "development" was seen to be a positive one embodying notions of progress and betterment. Development was a good thing, but development has increasingly become a dirty word - a reality which has condemned the majority of the world's population to poverty and inequality.

For most people development is defined in economic terms - it is measured, by economists, as Gross National Product per capita. A country and its people are "developed" if they have a high GNP per capita [Switzerland $16,330, the U.S. £15,390 in 1984] and "underdeveloped" if it is low [Ethiopia $110, Bangladesh $130]. Development is something which has been achieved in the West. But this development does not admit to the inequality in the distribution of wealth, property, services and ultimately life chances for many. The assumption that if economic growth can be achieved, development will follow has been shown to be false. By today's definition of development the rich get richer, the poor poorer and the absolute poor of the Third World die.

The reality of development today means that:

- approximately 800 million people live in absolute poverty.

- 400-500 million suffer chronic malnutrition.

- every day 40,000 children die a silent death.

- in 1979 Europe imported more than twice as much food from the Third World as it sent there.

- in 1983 the EEC destroyed 5 million kilos of fruit and vegetables every day. This equals 7% of total production.

This inequality is one threat to world peace and survival. Another comes from the threat to our environment that current development strategies entail. World resources are being consumed at an alarming rate not, as is often assumed, by the poor but by the rich. The recently published Brandt Report noted that one American uses as much commercial energy as two Germans or Australians, three Swiss or Japanese, six Yugoslavs, nine Mexicans, 16 Chinese, 19 Malaysians, 53 Indians or Indonesians, 109 Sri Lankans, 438 Malians, or 1070 Nepalese.

In the poor world the environmental crisis means that families cut down forests, overcultivate soil and overgraze pasture because they have no choice if they want to survive. In the rich world the environmental crisis means pollution, the hazards of nuclear energy and the manipulation of nature because we cannot or will not think of an alternative.

In this section the cartoons highlight many different approaches to development. We use them to raise questions about the patterns and processes which shape the world today. It is important to see these questions in the context of our own society as well as at a global level.

At the end of this section there is a collection of cartoons which make use of the basic shape of the globe in their design. They can provide a useful stimulus for people to draw their own.

Development: what do we mean?

All the cartoons in this section make a comment on the relationship between different groups of people in the world and the nature of development.

As an introduction to discussing these ideas it would be useful to ask people to select six cartoons and look at them closely.

- What points do you think the cartoonists are making?
- What are the detailed features of the cartoons which suggest these ideas?
- What do they use to symbolize their ideas?

An activity of this type also provides an opportunity for a group to become more aware of their basic assumptions and attitudes, which is an important starting point for more detailed discussion.

You could take this further by offering groups a selection of cartoons from which they are each asked to choose one which, for them, says something important about the nature of development. They can then explain their choice to each other and clarify the ideas they have in common as well as those they disagree about.

R Cobb Australia

NEWS

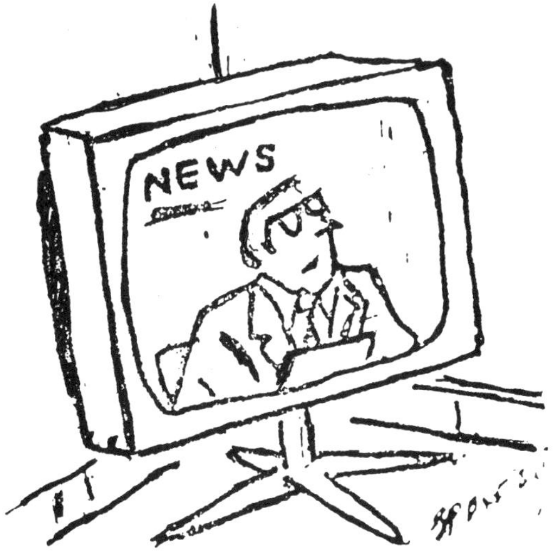

Spencer Britain

"Now, here are the news headlines again, with subtitles for viewers who are unable to believe their ears."

McKALE

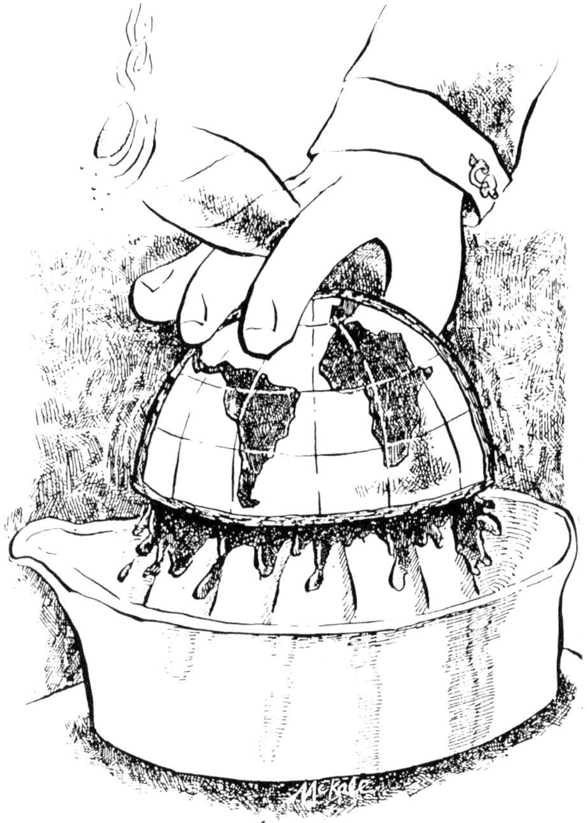

McKale USA

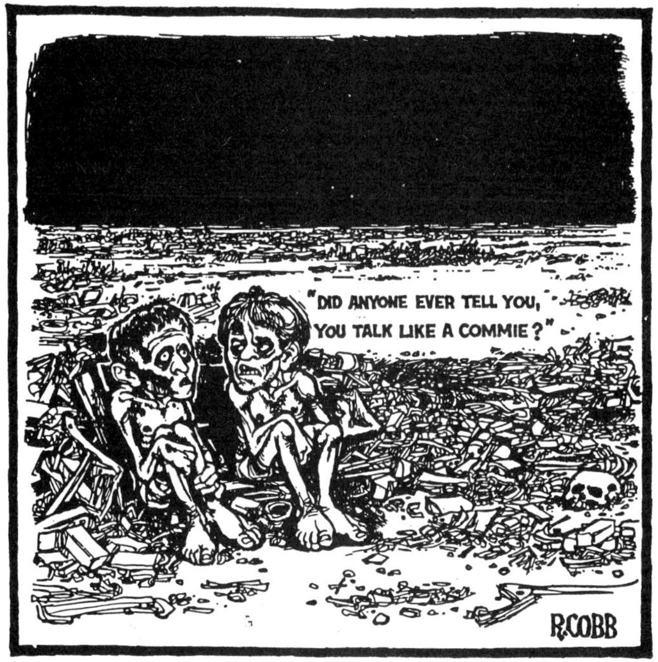

"DID ANYONE EVER TELL YOU, YOU TALK LIKE A COMMIE?"
R.COBB

R. Cobb Australia

"My programme is to increase harvests, cure the economy and get some statues made."

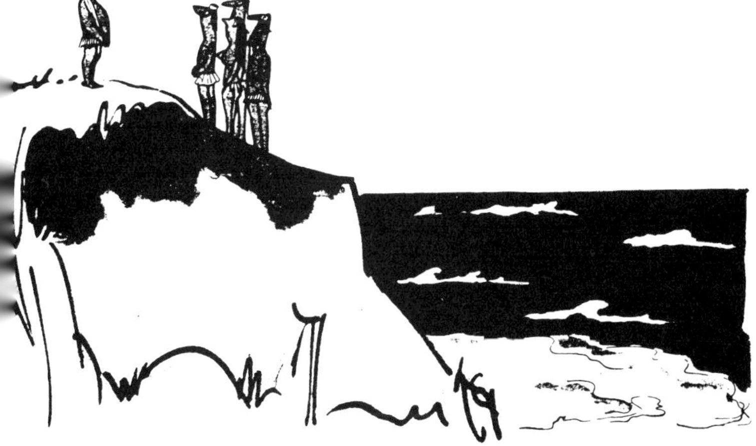

Ffolkes Britain

SAFARI HOLS
BIG MAC
EN 24 HOURS

"My God, you're right – it isn't a mirage."

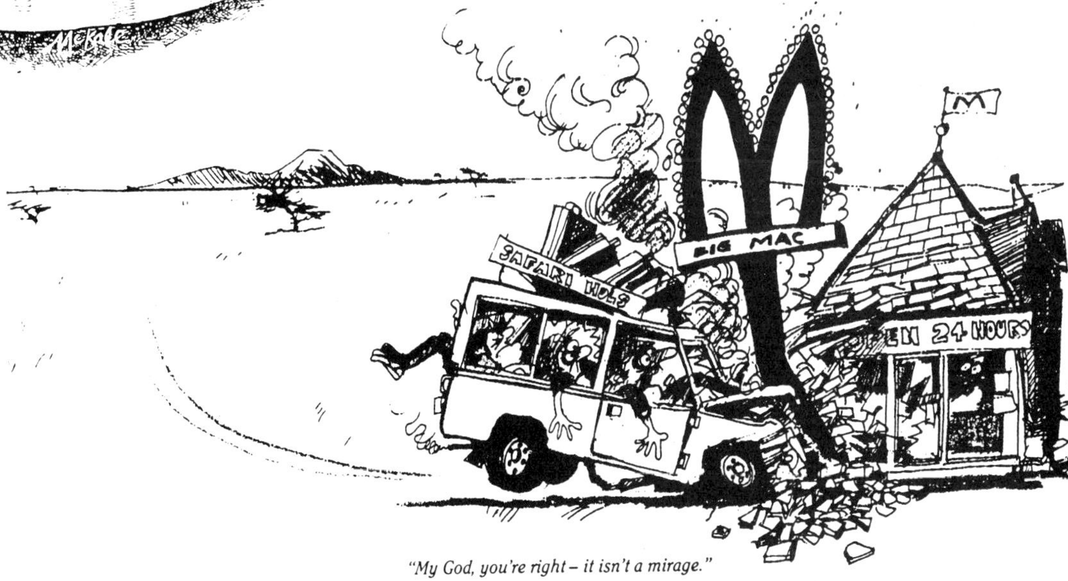

Dickinson Britain

Rachid Ait-Kaci Morocco

Laxman India

Of course we have progressed a great deal, first they were coming by bullock-cart, then by jeep — and now this!

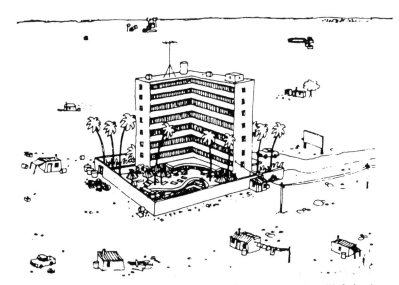

"*Dear George, here we are in the middle of things having a great time. We feel we're really getting to know this exotic country...*"

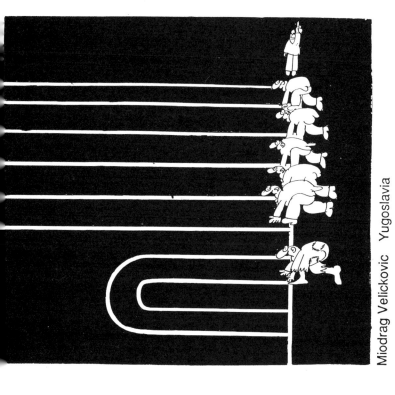

Miodrag Velickovic   Yugoslavia

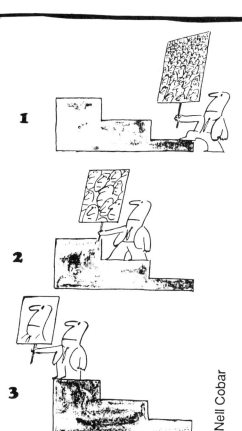

1

2

3

Nell Cobar

"I sometimes wish that I, too, were working for myself, and not just for humanity."

Handelsman USA

Quaker Peace & Serv.   Britain

For some groups it may be useful to organise this response in a way that can be followed up by further work. Each group could for example be given a large sheet of paper with the heading "Development is.......". They could then brainstorm as many endings to the sentence as they can think of. They can then be asked to mark those that all members of the group agree with and those about which there is disagreement. Alternatively, you could use the example below as a starting point.

Development is ....

- the fairer distribution of wealth.

- increased political stability.

- increased economic growth.

- a healthier, happier and more meaningful life for everyone.

- less dependence by one nation on another.

- the provision of basic needs for all.

- increased interdependence between nations.

- the availability of consumer goods.

De La Torre Mexico

'Here, Señor Carter, is the statue of Simón Bolívar, who liberated Latin America from foreign domination!'

Simpson USA

Expose...

EXTORT

STEAL

PILFER

SWIPE

GLUT

TAKE

BIG OIL

Mike Peters USA

.. THE CORPORATE GIANTS.

J. F. Batellier France

27

In dialogue?

A useful activity could focus on discussing the issues raised here and then asking people to suggest additions they would want to make to the selection. What kind of points would they be seeking to highlight?

Each of these cartoons relates to specific situations, for example Corax is making a comment on North South trade negotiations. As an introduction it is important to look at the detail of cartoons and to discuss some of the issues they raise. However, a selection of this type lends itself well to stimulating a wider discussion on how a group see, or indeed experience, the processes of dialogue and political change.

It is always important to select cartoons for use with groups which are appropriate for them as well as the work they are doing. The cartoon by Rashid Ait Kali could, in some contexts, simply be a stimulus to reinforcing a rather limited view of Islamic societies as seen from outside. We do however, have to be careful to avoid rejecting other people's caricaturing or questioning of the values of their own society because this is not a positive image in our view.

One of the central challenges which development education is about is how to avoid simply replacing one simplistic analysis with another albeit, in some peoples' view, more "enlightened" one!

Corax Yugoslavia

Kal Britain

THE PRESENT GOVERNMENT MAY BE CORRUPT

DICTATORIAL

OPPRESSIVE

BUT AT LEAST IT IS NOT COMMUNIST!

Rachid Ait-Kaci   Morocco

Carl Rose   USA

"I think I may say, without fear of contradiction . . ."

Plantu   France

Bo Brown   USA

'That's a good question which demands some real evasion.'

In our mutual interests?

In 1980 The Brandt Report entitled 'North - South: a Programme for Survival' was published. It put forward a number of key ideas for creating a more just world. It stated:

"We do not believe that mutual interests alone provide an adequate basis for all the changes that are needed. Especially as far as the poorest countries are concerned, the principal motives for our proposals are human solidarity and a commitment to international social justice. There must be an end to deprivation and suffering. It cannot be accepted that in one part of the world most people live relatively comfortably, while in another they struggle for sheer survival. As we shall argue, there are material reasons for trying to end this state of affairs - international political stability, expanding export markets, the preservation of the biological environment, the limitation of population growth. But we speak of solidarity as something that goes beyond mutual interests.

Mutual interests also do not provide a sufficient basis for change in the uses of economic power in the world, which we believe to be essential. The 'haves' are rarely willing to relinquish their control and their resources and share them with the 'have-nots'. Naturally there are conflicts between North and South; the most fundamental being questions of power and the numerous ways in which economic and even military strength confers on countries, organisations and corporations in the North the ability to manage the world economy to a considerable degree in its own favour"

Corax Yugoslavia

'GOT ANY CHANGE TO SPARE, MR. ARAB?'

'I'D RATHER NOT GET INVOLVED!'

'...SO YOU SEE, THE ENTIRE FUTURE OF THE INTERNATIONAL FINANCIAL SYSTEM HINGES ON YOUR CAPACITY FOR QUICK RECOVERY AND VAST ECONOMIC GROWTH.'

Oliphant   USA

The Brandt Report goes on to state that the areas where mutual interests between North and South exist include:

- expanding world trade and markets to everyone's benefit

- access to each other's markets for both developing and developed countries

- the proper global management of energy use, environment management and food production

- the mutual control of multinational companies

- the balanced and fair development of the international financial system

The Report concludes......
"Concern for the future of the planet is inextricably connected with concern about poverty. Continued rapid population growth in the next century could make the world unmanageable; but that growth can only be forestalled if action is taken to combat poverty in this century. Much the same is true for the biological environment, which is threatened with destruction in many countries as a direct result of poverty - though in others as a result of ill-considered technological decisions and patterns of industrial growth. These problems -nuclear weapons proliferation is another - can only be resolved by North and South acting in cooperation, and their mutual interests in doing so are only too obvious. The conquest of poverty and the promotion of sustainable growth are matters not just of the survival of the poor, but of everyone".

- Which cartoons, here or in other sections, relate to these mutual interests?

An issue agenda
- *Energy and development*

Cartoons can also be a very useful stimulus for motivating a group to build up a list of some issues which can then form the basis for planning further discussion.

In a similar way to the brainstorming activity already suggested, this also gives an opportunity to find out more about the starting points in a group - the assumptions and understanding individuals bring to their work on a new subject.

The cartoons on the next four pages are all on the theme of energy.

- What issues do they refer to?
- How do they relate to different approaches to development?
- Who might disagree with the views of the cartoonists? Why?

Questions such as these make a useful start to building up an agenda. It is also vital to ask what are the other issues, about energy and development, not shown in the cartoons. The discussion could then be focused by suggesting that each small group draws up a list of questions which relate to the issues which need to be followed up.

Martyn Turner   Ireland

McLachlan   Britain

"*Poor devils—another year under the threat of nuclear war.*"

PROPOSAL: SITE FOR NUCLEAR PLANT THAT WILL CONVINCE US THAT SUCH THINGS CAN BE CLEAN AND SAFE.

Martyn Turner [after Kinney USA]

Steve Greenberg USA

REASON FOR SOME CONCERN

COULD BE WORSE

REASONABLE

NOT THE BEST

SLIGHTLY UNACCEPTABLE

ACCEPTABLE LEVEL OF RADIATION

UNOFFICIAL SCIENTIFIC REPORT

TANDBERG

Ron Tandberg Australia

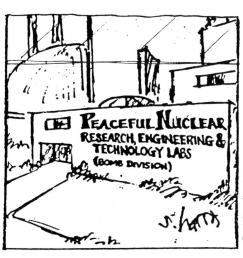

PEACEFUL NUCLEAR
RESEARCH, ENGINEERING &
TECHNOLOGY LABS
(BOMB DIVISION)

S. Harris USA

HOW WOULD SIR LIKE HIS TWENTIETH CENTURY?

I'LL HAVE THE BURNT BITS AT EACH END

Cook Australia

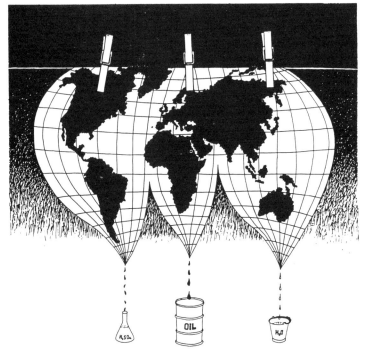

Baculev Bulgaria

OPEC

Garner USA

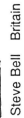

Steve Bell Britain

"ANYTHING EXCITING HAPPEN AT THE NUCLEAR POWER PLANT TODAY?"

Phil Frank

AND THE WEST DOESN'T HAVE ANY REACTORS OF SIMILAR DESIGN TO THE RUSSIAN ONE...

Ours are like Three Mile Island

FURTHERMORE OUR NUCLEAR INSTALLATIONS HAVE SOPHISTICATED COMPUTER CONTROLLED SAFETY DEVICES...

...Like N.A.S.A. had for The Challenger...

AND THEREFORE A SPOKESMAN HAS STATED, THERE IS NO CAUSE FOR PANIC OR ALARM... ...GOODNIGHT...

Martyn Turner   Ireland

Throwaway Planet

Engelhardt   USA

STANLEY

BY Murray Ball.

OKAY JACKSON, SO I'M WHITE AND YOU'RE BLACK...

...SO WHAT DIFFERENCE DOES THAT MAKE? WE ALL CONTRIBUTE TO SOCIETY!

I MEAN EACH GROUP HAS RECEIVED SOMETHING FROM THE OTHERS...

YEH.

...WE GOT YOUR LAWS AND YOU GOT OUR LAND...

Murray Ball New Zealand

How do you see the world?

Cartoons based on maps, even if only in a loose sense, can be very expressive in highlighting views. An activity to draw a "mental map" of how people see schools, shops or the local police station can be the starting point for very valuable discussion.

The cartoons on the next few pages are all based on the theme of the globe. They could be used for a number of the activities suggested in the introduction but they also make a good starting point for suggesting that people draw their own cartoon. Less emphasis should be given to artistic skill than to attempting to sum up some notion of how you see the world. Alternatively suggest that groups work together to draw a few cartoons showing how they imagine someone else, the President of the USA or Premier of USSR for example, sees the shape of the world.

What future?

On pages 40 -41 there are three cartoons which beg the question - what future? What are the cartoons saying to you? What questions are the cartoonists attempting to raise?

The cartoon from Rumania suggests that the world has to make a choice. A useful discussion could focus on this.

- What are the choices?
- Are there others?
- What symbols would you put on the hands to represent the choices you see as important?

It is valuable to use a limited number of cartoons to start off a broad discussion of this nature.

MUNDO CRUEL

Pedro Sol   Mexico

Yayo   Colombia

Hankour   Algeria

Corax   Yugoslavia

THE WORLD. MERCATOR'S PROJECTION

REAGAN'S PROJECTION

Evans   Britain

DEW   Trinidad

WHA'PPEN!

Brick   Britain

TO LET SUIT AMBITIOUS AMOEBA

Brick   Britain

MIDDLE EAST

R. Cobb   Australia

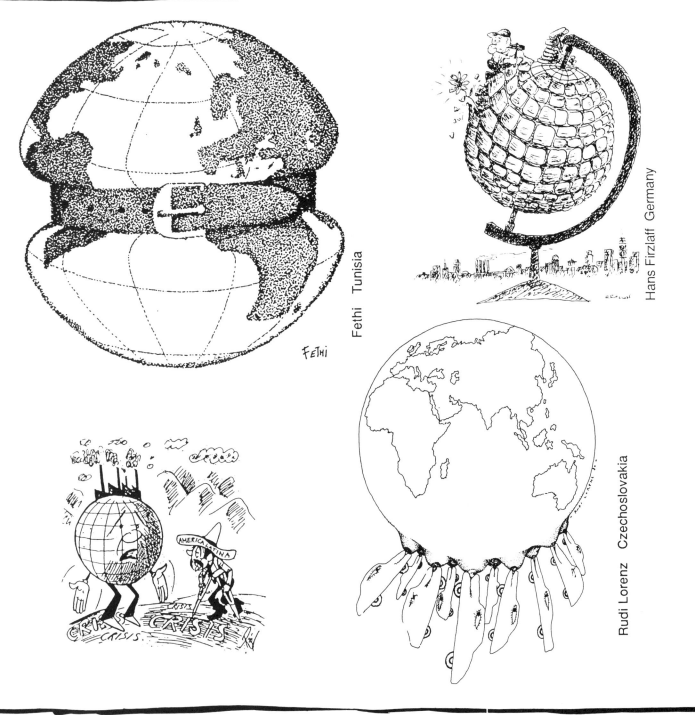

Fethi Tunisia

Hans Firzlaff Germany

Rudi Lorenz Czechoslovakia

Tokoro Japan

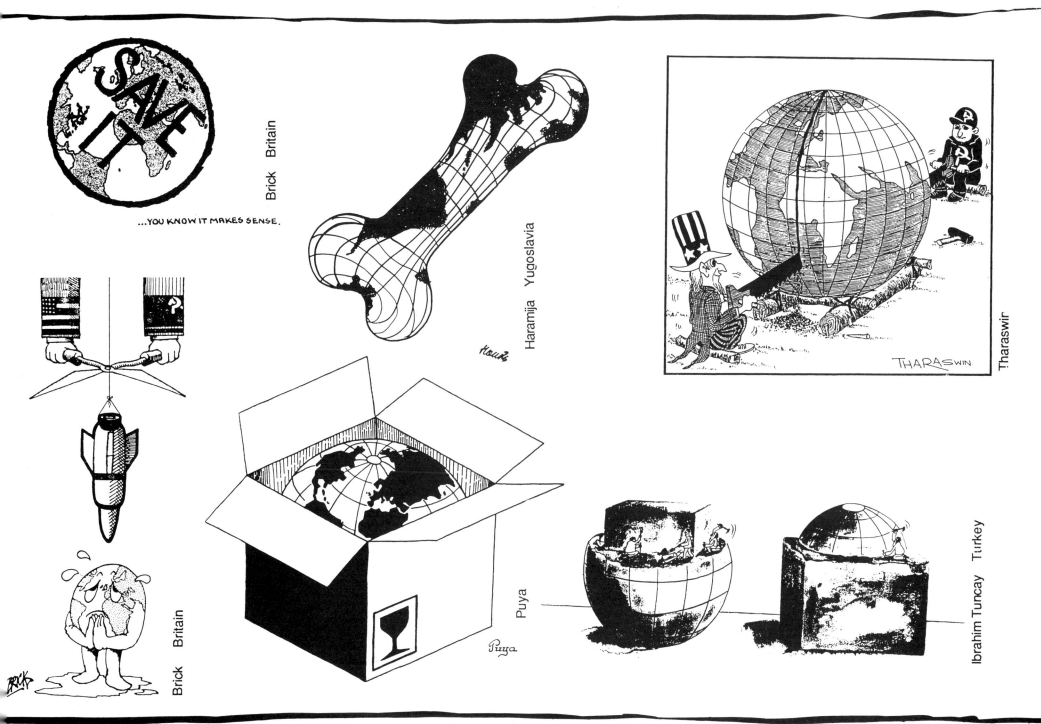

...YOU KNOW IT MAKES SENSE.

Brick   Britain

Brick   Britain

Haramija   Yugoslavia

Puya

Tharaswin

Ibrahim Tuncay   Turkey

Ajubel   Cuba

Seckin   Turkey

To read

North-South: A Programme for Survival
[Brandt Commission, Pan, 1980.]
A very useful, wide ranging, easily available guide to some of the principle issues.

The Cruel Choice
[Denis Goulet, Athenum, 1971.]
A brilliant, philosophical but eminently practical and readable account of the moral debates surrounding development.

Inside the Third World
[Paul Harrison, Penguin, 1979.]
Easily available survey of the main issues - complete with useful case studies, statistics and references.

Our Common Future
[World Commission on Environment and Development, OUP, 1987]
Best selling review of the key issues today - population, resources, ecology, energy, industry and urbanisation. Outlines a number of strategies for common action.

Down to Earth
[Eckholm, E., Pluto, 1982.]
Detailed review of some of the major ecological/environmental issues from a political economy perspective.

For teaching

Dialogue for Development: Handbook
[C. Regan et al, Trocaire, 1984.]
Teachers' handbook of ideas / activities and resources. Useful section on development education, what is it and why teach it.

BLOWING

MIND TEST

Get **X** to **Y** using only the entire technological resources of the Western World.

X

SURPLUS
USA

SURPLUS
EEC

Y
(WHY?)

We had seen similar pictures on our T.V. screens before - Kampuchea, Biafra, the Sahel, Ethiopia - but they didn't seem to have the same effect. Despite earlier accurate warnings and reports, dating back to 1982, the T.V. pictures presented by Michael Buerk and Mohammed Amin in November 1984 shocked the world. They revealed an unfolding crisis of horrific dimensions in Ethiopia - for a second the world stood still.

The dimensions of the crisis were immense - up to 8 million at risk in Ethiopia alone and up to 35 million "seriously at risk" in a further 22 African states according to the United Nations. Immediate food aid needs topped $400 million, transport needs over $50 million, non-food needs (health care, water supply, sanitation, agricultural inputs, refugee programmes) over $500 million. The crisis was all the more real because it unfolded on all our television sets.

The immediate response was huge - the over $80 million donated to the Band Aid Trust, the massive increases in voluntary agency funds, the increased food aid budgets, the emergency feeding programmes and airlifts, the pledges of governments [many still unrealised] and the new plans for the future. Again, the impact of the media ensured and galvanised action. Even so, over one million people died. As the reports filtered through, the aeroplanes lifted off and the food programmes began, the search for explanations started.

Why weren't we warned sooner? Why didn't the media report the crisis earlier? Surely the international and voluntary agencies knew in advance? Some argued that the crisis was the result of the policies of African governments and in Ethiopia due to the communist character of the regime which was more interested in dogma than development. Others argued that the crisis represented the failure of western development aid packages and the continued exploitation of the Third World for its commodities and resources. Still others pointed to the neglect of agriculture and of the needs of poor peasant farmers. The crisis was not just an Ethiopian or indeed an African crisis but was in fact a crisis of development. *How was it that after decades of development this could still happen? How was it that the moon had been conquered but not famine?* These questions remained largely unanswered.

Clearly the African food crisis was not just a crisis for the individual states involved but was also an international crisis for development.

This became all the more apparent when people began to equate our greed with their need [best exemplified over the past few years by the EEC's growing food mountain]. How was it that our part of the world paid for the storage of food and even penalised farmers for growing more while another part starved? Why wouldn't the transfer of our surplus solve the problem? All the time the questions went deeper and every time the same unease appeared - there were serious questions to be asked about this crisis and its origins and the answers were not being given.

In South Africa today, the reality of apartheid condemns the vast majority of people to third class status in their own land simply because of the colour of their skin. Apartheid threatens not only the future of South Africa but of Southern Africa as a whole. In the ensuing tension the two superpowers align with their allies and extend the crisis beyond Southern Africa. Apartheid represents a crisis which threatens us all morally or strategically.

In Nicaragua, in Central America; in Chile, in South America; in the Lebanon, throughout the Middle East, crises recur. They are not regional crises but world crises - crises of geopolitics of which we are all a part. Global economics and politics admit no bystanders. If there is a third world war it will probably begin in the Third World.

The spark is less likely to arise from the strategic conflicts of either the United States or the Soviet Union per se, but rather from the extreme poverty of this part of the world. The economic condition of 75% of the world's people threatens to affect us all. World peace and prosperity increasingly hinge on events in the Third World.

As well as this recent events demonstrate the direct and immediate relevance of events thousands of miles away. The American bombing of Tripoli in April 1986, the disaster in the Chernobyl nuclear plant gave a new and terrifying meaning to the term interdependence.

The food crisis in Africa, the political and military crises in South Africa, Central America and the Middle East, the economic crisis of the Third World and of the developed world and the environmental crisis highlighted by Chernobyl are moral crises, which affect us all.

This section starts by using cartoons to explore different images of famine and the notion of guilt about famine. This is followed up by exploring famine in its global, social, economic and political context.

The section concludes by asking the question, Whose crisis? using cartoons about Central America and on the theme of debt as examples.

Hunger in the world

Cartoons are not jokes, they are often not funny, especially when they capture some of the irony and scandal of the things we allow to happen in this world. The famine in Ethiopia [1984-5] eventually received considerable media focus.

We may feel guilty but how often do we see ourselves as part of the problem, part of the cause? The politics and economics of the West have a lot to answer for, but it is our sense of guilt which can all too often get in the way of seeing the issues. It is useful to provide opportunities for people to explore their ideas on the notion of such guilt.

Offer groups a collection of cartoons showing different aspects of famine.

- What images do they suggest?
- How do they <u>feel</u> about them?
- Do they show the whole picture?
- What should our response be to this?
- What lessons should have been learnt by the experience of Ethiopia?
- Do you think they have been?

Kal Britain

On a clear day you can see ETHIOPIA...

Calman Britain

"Would you like to be left alone to feel guilty about Ethiopia before or after the sweet trolley?"

McAllistar Britain

ETHIOPIE 84

EEC FOOD MOUNTAIN

SUDAN

ETHIOPIA

NEVER MIND, CHILDREN – I EXPECT THEY NEED IT ALL FOR THEMSELVES

Bill Caldwell   Britain

WESTERN AID

BEST BEFORE: YESTERDAY.

Peter Brookes   Britain

WATER!

Nasser   Egypt

POLITICS

ETHIOPIA FAMINE AID

Kal   Britain

Libyan Calendar

Responding to famine

Cartoonists often manage to draw links between events in a way which sharpens up the issues which politicians all too often want to cloud over. The cartoons on the next few pages and on pages 44-45, all comment on responses to famine. They raise a wide range of issues which can provide a focus for useful group discussion and the start of further work to investigate the nature of a more responsible response to famine in the world today.

As an introduction ask people to work in pairs discussing the cartoons and getting an overview of the whole collection. Then bring the group together to brainstorm the issues they feel the cartoonists are attempting to raise.

This approach provides the opportunity for discussing the complex issue of famine in the context of other issues, themselves equally complex, but at the same time clarifies the need for quite basic questions........

Is famine to do with lack of food - with climatic problems or to do with politics? You can see Ethiopia on a clear day - but how clearly? Does the very energy and concern that goes into responding to the need for aid divert us from understanding what is going on? Is the main response ... aid ... then conferences ... words ......until it happens again?

How many times does it have to happen? We have the technology to go to the moon but not to pull the plough? How was this decided? Is this our political priority?

Bread not bombs. Why are arms such a priority? Is the world food issue a political time bomb? Does the ideological fear of politicians in the North stop them from listening to the needs of the South? What is it they fear?

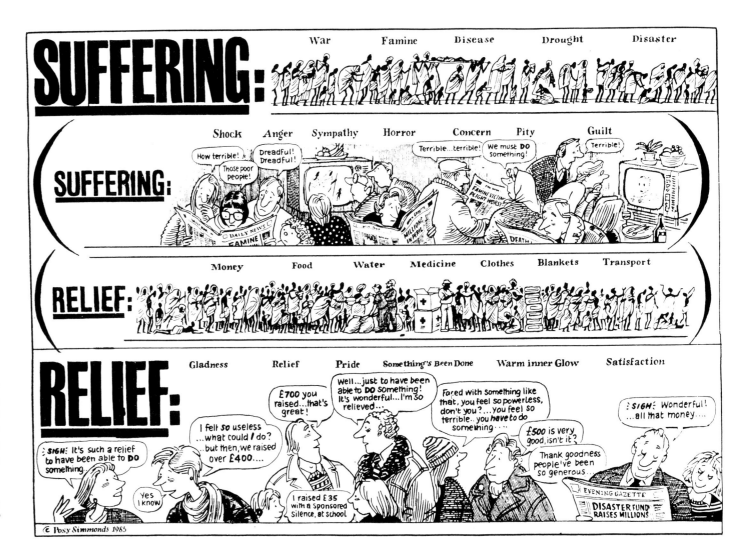

Plantu France

World Food Conference

MENU

AUTH

Auth USA

Sorry old boy ...

but charity begins ...

...at home

Oh that's fine

—if you've got a home

Ian Kellas Britain

"They feed people with words ..."

Plantu France

Bucchi Italy

Heath Britain

Mick Jagger tucks microphone down the front of his pants and claps his hands. This will support one Ethiopian family for twenty years.

Mick rubs his hand up Tina Turner's thigh accompanied by pelvic jerking...buys eighteen truck loads of wheat, enough to support an entire Ethiopian village for two years.

Leunig Australia

JIM BORGMAN ©1984 CINCINNATI ENQUIRER KING FEATURES

Plantu France

Jim Borgman USA

Naji al Ali   Lebanon

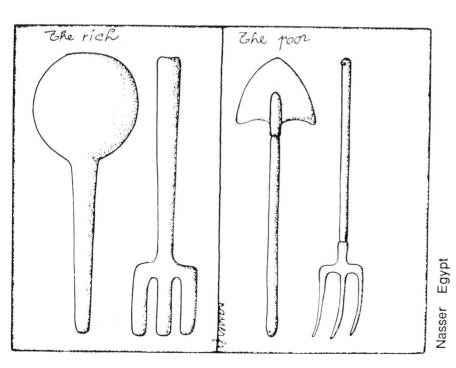

The rich

The poor

Nasser   Egypt

Bordeclerc   France

49

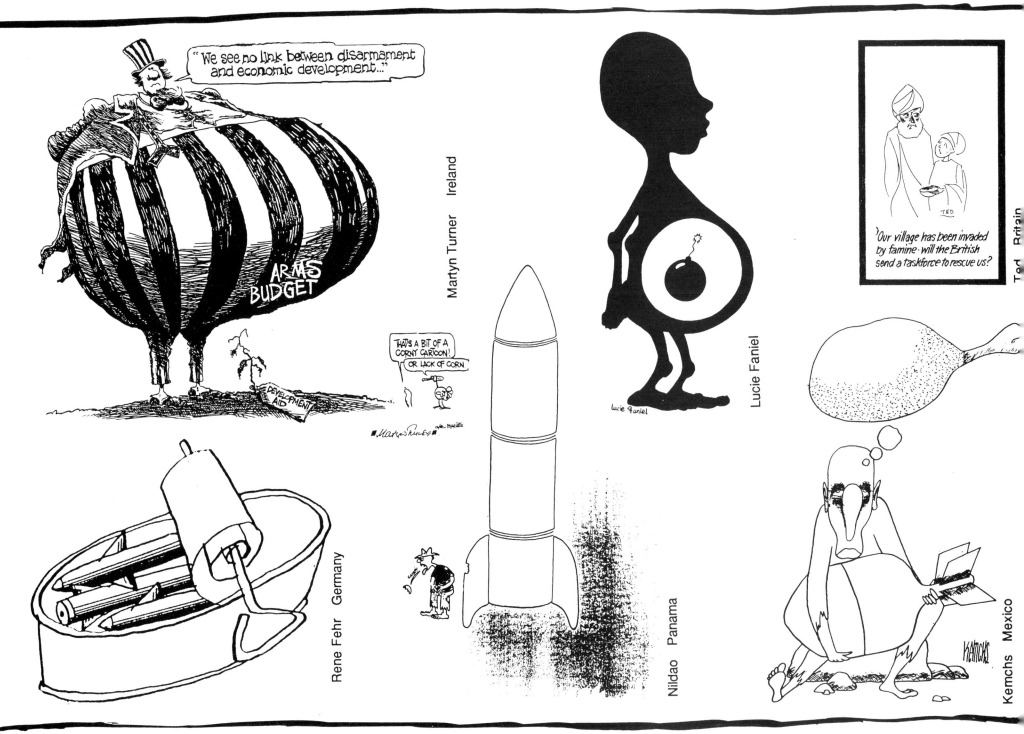

50

Naji al Ali   Lebanon

Yayo   Colombia

"Trouble Spots"

This section raises the question 'Whose Crisis?' in the context of Central America and the Debt Crisis.

The first collection of cartoons are all on the theme of Central America and its relationship with the USA. What do the cartoons suggest about this relationship?

It may be useful to review the cartoons and note the main features of the relationship, then read the extract on page 54 *from Central America Comment [CIIR , London, l987].*

It may then be useful to look at the cartoons again .... Do you see them differently?

• What is the nature of the crisis?
• How do you think the USA relates to what is happening?

The cartoons on pages 56-57 are about Third World debt. In what way do the cartoons suggest that the Third World debt crisis is a <u>world</u> debt crisis? What do the cartoons suggest would happen if Third World countries defaulted?

The cartoons on pages 58-59 introduce other issues which seem to be a crisis for some but not for others, or crises which are presented as trouble spots rather than issues which we are all involved in.

These cartoons, along with others from this book, can be used as a stimulus to brainstorm 'crises' which appear to be localised but have wider consequences. An outline world map could be used to collate the information.

Carol Simpson   Australia

52

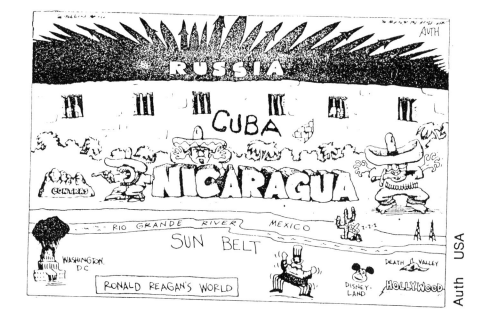

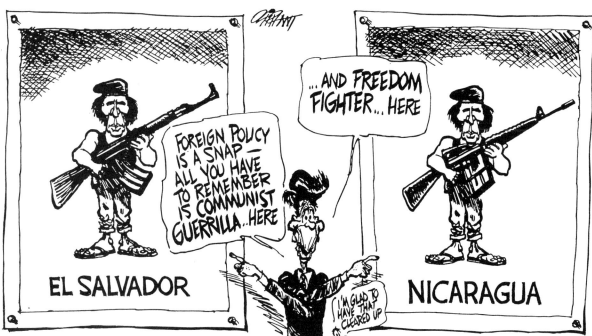

"The possibilities of a peaceful solution in Central America rest crucially with the United States.....

The civilian governments of El Salvador and Guatemala are held back by traditional vested interests - the military, business and, in El Salvador, by the United States itself - from entering into negotiations which might lead to a peaceful resolution of civil war. Throughout the 1980s the United States has worked to make Honduras and Costa Rica accomplices in the war against Nicaragua.

By presenting the challenge of change in Central America in terms of the East-West conflict, the Reagan administration has obscured the real issues that have given rise to unrest and instability in the region. The problems facing Central America today remain those of poverty, landlessness and injustice.

Throughout this century, Central Americans who have tried to reform or radically change these systems have met with resistance from the privileged and powerful few, supported invariably by the United States. In 1987 the Reagan administration is intending to spend $1,2286m to support its allies in Central America and up to $500m on the 'contra' war against Nicaragua. The administration sees the destabilisation of Nicaragua and the maintenance of the status quo elsewhere in the region as a test of its political will. The US public, when questioned in opinion polls, has shown little support for its government's militaristic policies in Central America. The insistence on seeing the Central American conflicts in crude East-West terms has also been met with scepticism by ideologically diverse European and Latin American governments.

What is certain is that there will be no lasting peace in the region until the United States respects the efforts of Central Americans themselves to bring about the social changes required to improve their lives. The different strands of Christianity, Nationalism and Marxism will, as in Nicaragua, continue to inspire revolutionary movements to seek remedies for the region's deeply rooted injustices and build a fairer society. The continued funding of counter-insurgency and counter-revolution, in their many forms, can only prolong the suffering of the peoples of Central America.

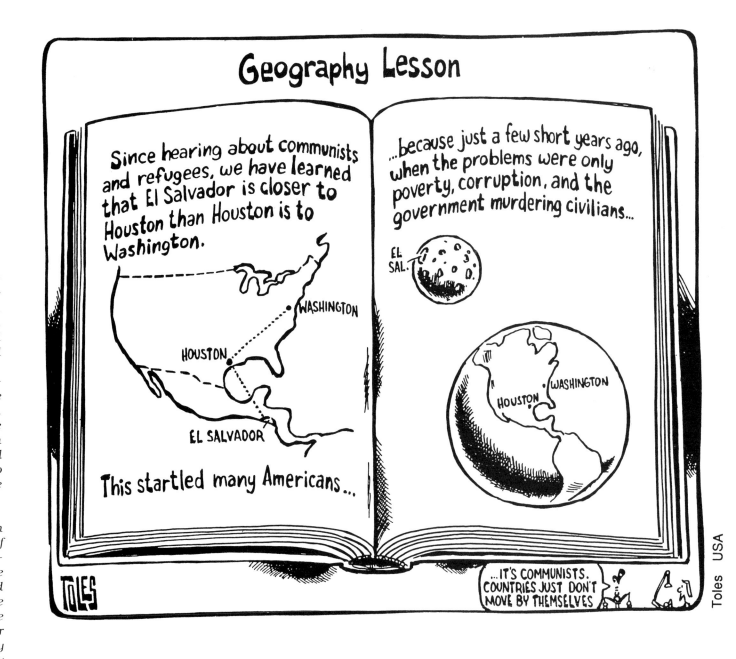

'YOU'RE OBVIOUSLY SUFFERING FROM AN ACUTE MILITARY AID DEFICIENCY!'

Oliphant USA

♪ "WE ARM THE WORLD..." ♪

Jim Borgman USA

'SENOR CASTRO EXPORTS HIS REVOLUTION, AND SENOR REAGAN EXPORTS HIS ECONOMIC THEORIES...
WHY IS EVERYBODY INTENT ON DESTROYING US?'

Oliphant USA

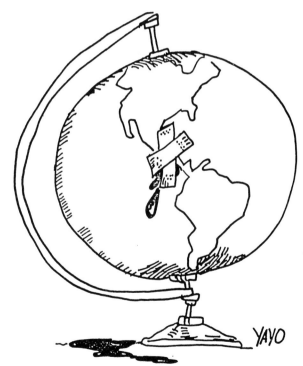

Yayo Colombia

Heavily indebted countries [1984]

1 = Debt, US$bn.
2 = Debt, %GNP
3 = GNP/Capita US$

	1.	**2.**	**3.**
Argentina	38.1	46.8	2230
Brazil	87.2	44.0	1720
Chile	17.2	100.2	1700
Mexico	87.5	54.2	2040
Morocco	10.6	79.9	670
Nigeria	12.7	17.0	730
Peru	11.3	68.2	1000
Philippines	14.1	43.9	660
Venezuela	23.7	52.7	3410
Yugoslavia	17.0	42.2	2120

Source: *North South Issue paper.*
[Trocaire, Dublin 1987]

The figures above hide one important aspect of the world debt crisis - its impact on the poorest countries especially those of Africa, south of the Sahara. Though that region's total debt is small in world terms, it is huge in relation to its ability to pay. Debt repayments those countries form a higher percentage of GDP than they do in Latin America.

Martyn Turner Ireland

Wasserman USA

USA monopolies are keeping the countries of Latin America in perpetual servitude — their common foreign debt has reached 360 million dollars.

Uncle Sam to a Latin American: What are you dissatisfied with — I'm giving you a lot of help, aren't I?

Drawing by V. Volkov.

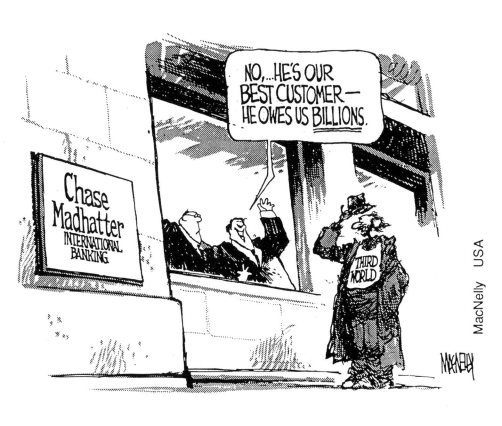

MacNelly USA

Ken Alexander USA

Wasserman USA

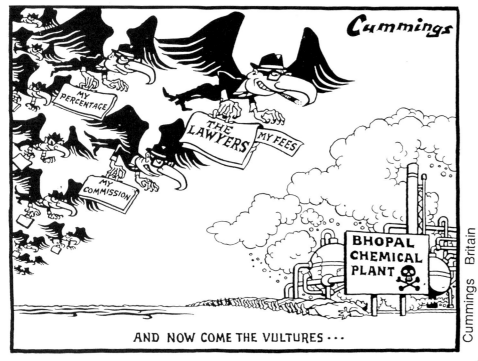

AND NOW COME THE VULTURES...

Cummings Britain

Your analysis is wrong! I'll explain. The U.S. expects India to tell the U.S.S.R. to influence Pakistan to pressurise the U.S. to make the U.S.S.R. warn China—

Laxman India

Bruce Petty Australia

Rob Lawlor USA

Fine, thanks . . . how's the energy crisis with you?'

Szep USA

MacNelly USA

To read

The Real Cost
[Richard North, Chatto and Windus, 1986.]
An illustrated , large format review of food, environment and development issues. Contains many case studies of various commodities - bread, tea, bananas, cigarettes, gold, cars etc.

Central American Comment
[Catholic Institute for Int. Relations, 1987.]
Cheap, up to date and accurate review of the main issues and challenges today.

For teaching

Food Matters
[Trocaire, Dublin and B'ham DEC, 1987.]
Student book on food in the world today. Looks at nutrition, human rights, causes of hunger. It uses a case study of Ethiopia.

Disasters in the Classroom: Teaching about disasters in the Third World
[Oxfam, 1986.]
Pack of exercises, activities and stimulus materials for tackling classroom teaching.

Learning about El Salvador
[Andes Support Group, 1985]
Excellent and systematic exploration of the issues and debates plus specific ideas and materials for introducing El Salvador in a learning context.

Dealing with Debt: A Teaching Resource
[Save the Children, 1987.]
Comprehensive pack dealing with debt and related issues at personal, national and international level.

Guns, Bombs and Butter

Speaking at the World Food Conference in 1974, the Vice-President of the United States, Dr. Henry Kissinger, made a famous speech.

"...today we must proclaim a bold objective - that within a decade no child will go to bed hungry, that no family will fear for its next day's bread, that no human being's future and capacities will be stunted by malnutrition.... Let the nations gathered here resolve to confront the challenge..."

In 1984 UNICEF, the United Nations Children's Fund, calculated that 40,000 children under five years of age, were dying every day. Between 1984 and 1986 over one million people died of starvation and related diseases in Sudan and Ethiopia alone. In 1986 the amount spent on arms for that year was over $1000 billion.

It is said that a balance in the stockpile of weapons both nuclear and conventional makes the world a safer place and has brought peace. It is easy to forget the more than 140 wars which have taken place, mostly in the Third World, since 1945. Millions of people are condemned to lives of poverty and misery because resources are "scarce" or because the superpowers fight out their battles in other peoples' lands. It is easy to forget the conflicts in the Middle East, Central America, South Africa etc. which are made all the more horrific because the weapons are all the more sophisticated. Can there be peace while there is mass hunger and mass poverty? Is peace just the absence of war?

We speak of scarce resources, public spending cuts and balance of payments problems, whilst military spending continues to use up labour, land, raw materials, research skills and brainpower as well as industrial capacity. The value of the weapons we sell to the Third World far outstrips the value of our "aid". We can send people to the moon, while others are condemned to death by starvation.

The $1000 billion which will be spent in 1986 on arms is a vindication of Albert Einstein's statement that the atomic bomb has changed everything except the minds and thinking of people.

In July 1986 newspapers carried two parallel stories. One recorded the fact that arms spending between 1960 and 1980 had increased by over 800%. The other witnessed the reopening of two major disarmament conferences, one the 35 Nation Conference on Disarmament in Europe had involved 30 months of "fruitless talking", the other the UN Disarma-

ment Conference was, after 24 years, "bogged down" on the issue of chemical weapons. The talks continue, the impasse remains, the arms race is real.

Today the number of nuclear weapons in the world is estimated to be 40,000 - 45,000. Their destructive power is a million times that of the Hiroshima bomb.

Even relatively small amounts of the funds now spent on arms could be used to eradicate misery:

- Today 50% of the Third World lacks clean water and sanitation. Through providing water taps and appropriate sewage systems, the rate of typhoid, dysentery, cholera and eye diseases could be halved. The cost, over a decade, would be $7 billion.

- The military expenditure of half a day would be enough to finance the World Health Organisation's programme to eradicate malaria.

- The cost of one modern tank could improve the storage facilities for 100,000 tons of rice, so that annual wastage of 4,000 tons or more could be avoided - a day's ration for eight million people.

- The price of a jet fighter could set up 40,000 village health centre.

The basic human needs are there, the political will to tackle them is not. The historian R.H. Tawney once suggested that militarism was not a characteristic of an army but rather of a society. The morality of present world society is clearly shown in its promotion of and fascination with the technology of death and its lack of consistent concern for the survival of life.

"...force alone does not guarantee security... a nation can reach a point at which it does not buy more security for itself simply by buying more military hardware... Indeed, to the extent that such expenditure severely reduces the resources available for other essential sectors and social-services-and fuels a futile and reactive arms race-excessive military spending can erode security rather than enhance it".

Robert McNamara - World Bank

The main theme of this section is arms and development. It begins with a collection of cartoons which raise questions about our priorities. It then goes on to look at the "balance" between East and West. The section concludes with a collection of "dove" cartoons and invites you to draw your own.

The cartoons on the next few pages all question the priority given to the "defence" and the attitudes which influence this situation. As an introductory activity, suggest that small groups review the cartoons and develop a key word or short phrase for each cartoon. These can then be shared with the whole group. This can provide the basis for a full discussion which starts from the different interpretations.

These cartoons do not offer many arguments for the build up of arms and the priority for defence. A useful activity could centre on groups identifying the kind of images and ideas which might be portrayed by arguing for defence policies.

Willy Lohmann   Holland

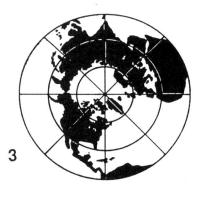

3

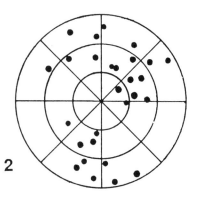

2

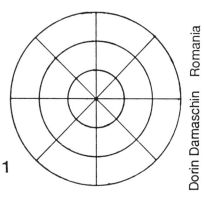

1

Dorin Damaschin   Romania

Amal Chakrabarti India

Yayo Colombia

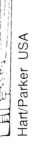

Hart/Parker USA

Brick Britain

63

Bill Cook Australia

Ane Vasilevski Yugoslavia

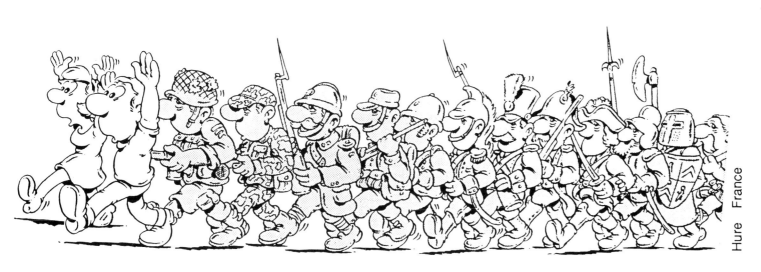

Hure France

"I'm absolutely against total war, but then I'm not for total peace either."

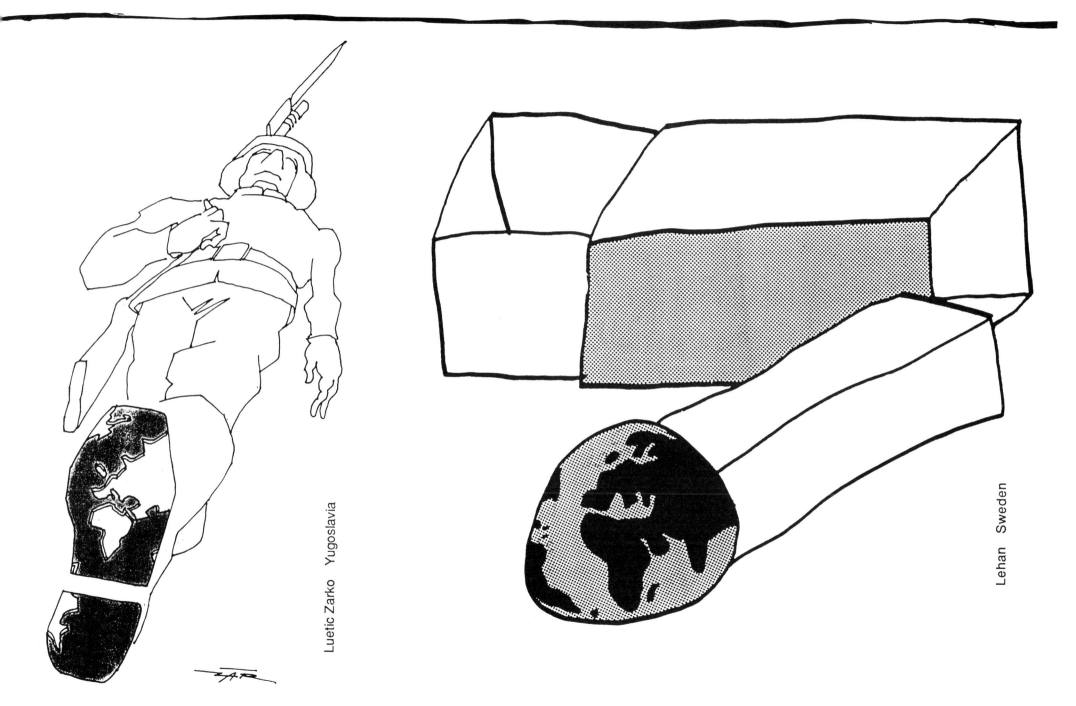

Luetic Zarko Yugoslavia

Lehan Sweden

65

Five minutes!

What are the three cartoons on this page saying about the state of the world?

- Is it five minutes to midnight? ......or do people in every age see that time must soon come to an end?

- What are the hands of the clock? Will the big hand on the clock move or the other one or is this not the situation at all?

- What are the marks on the starving child?

- On the cartoon opposite why are people's hands held high?

It is valuable to give time to close consideration of a few cartoons such as these. Discussion could be developed by using them in conjunction with the fable 'The history of a day'.

Floros Panagiotis Greece

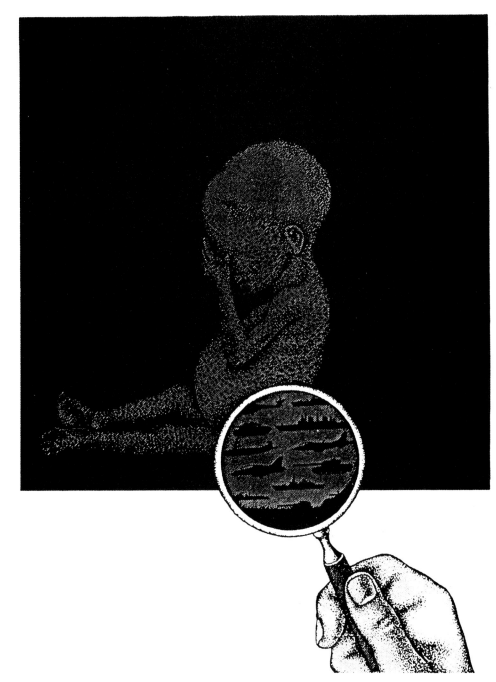

Zec Bulgaria

The history of a day

And then, on the stroke of midnight, the people had the world to themselves. For a long while, so far as we know, they were very quiet. All through the morning, and all through the afternoon, they just wandered around in small groups - hunting animals with spears and arrows, sheltering in caves, dressing themselves in skins. At about six o'clock in the evening they began to learn about seeds and manure and so on, and about how to herd and milk animals. By about half past seven some of them were living in biggish cities. This was mainly in Egypt and North India, and in the countries between.

Moses came and went at about a quarter to nine. Buddha in India, Socrates in Greece, Confucius in China, all came and went together, though they didn't know each other, at about ten past ten. Christ was about half past ten, as also, give or take a minute or so, were the Great Wall of China and Julius Caesar. Mahomet was at eleven.

At around half past eleven there began to be biggish cities in northern Europe. From about a quarter to twelve onwards people went out from these cities, and they began stealing from the rest of the world. They stole America, both North and South, they stole Northern Asia, they stole India, and just after four minutes to midnight they stole Africa. At about two minutes to midnight they had a big war amongst themselves, and then had another big war only 50 seconds later.

During the last minute before midnight these people from northern Europe were pushed back out of India and Africa, and also back out of many other countries, though not out of North America or Northern Asia, where they had become very settled indeed. Also during this last minute these people invented nuclear weapons, they landed on the moon, they were responsible for almost doubling the world's population, they used up more oil and more metal than had been used in all the previous 23 hours 59 minutes put together.

It was now midnight again. The start of a new day.

Let's play!

The cartoons on the next three pages all relate the arms issue to children and their future.

• What do they suggest about our values and our priorities for the future?

The statistics below show the life expectancy at birth and infant mortality rates [per 1,000 live births] for ·selected countries. What development expenditure could help to improve these figures? Why are these not a priority?

1 = Life Expectancy at Birth (Years) 1985
2 = Infant Mortality rate per 1,000 live births

Country	1.	2.
Ethiopia	41	152
Bangladesh	49	124
Kenya	54	76
China	69	36
Philippines	66	48
Zimbabwe	57	76
Guatemala	61	65
Brazil	64	67
Panama	72	25
Libya	60	90
Ireland	73	10
United Kingdom	74	10
USA	75	11
Bulgaria	72	16
USSR	72	24

Source: *UNICEF State of the World's Children.*

Jim Borgman   USA

LEATHERNECK!
WORKING REPLICA
OF FIGHTING U.S.
★ MARINE ★

PUTS YOU IN THE ACTION

R. COBB

R. Cobb   Australia

ACTION MAN
DESERTER

Clive Collins

DID YOUR PARENTS LET YOU WATCH THE TELEVISION SHOW ABOUT NUCLEAR WAR?

YEAH - AND THEY WERE THE ONES WHO GOT SCARED

WHAT PART MADE THEM SCARED?

THE PART WHEN I ASKED THEM WHAT THEY WERE GOING TO DO ABOUT IT

Wasserman   USA

LET'S PLAY STARWARS!
YOU BE THE ASH...

KogLer

Brian Kogler   Australia

CHILDREN!
STOP BEHAVING
LIKE ADULTS!

Heath   Britain

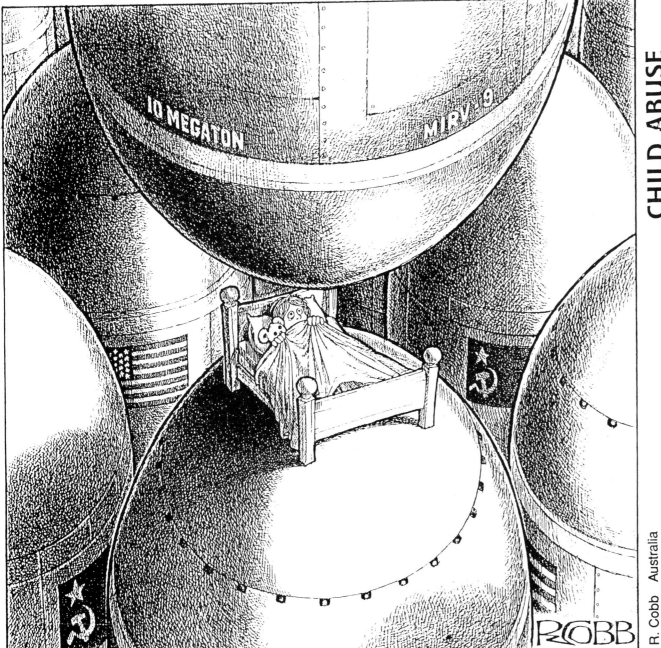

R. Cobb   Australia

CHILD ABUSE

When I grow up I want to be alive...

CALMAN

Calman   Britain

Quino Argentina

Images of war, power

The cartoons on the next three pages all raise issues about images of war and power. They all question underlying values. The cartoon on this page by Quino needs close examination:

• What are the symbols in part one and two of the cartoon? What do the statues represent?

• Why are they walking past?

• What are the symbols in part three?

• Why are they clearing it up?

• What is the cartoon suggesting about our values?

Discussion about values is often difficult to introduce, cartoons such as these can stimulate a wide range of reactions which can then be argued out in small groups.

A collection using some of these cartoons and some from pages 68-70 will provide a challenging agenda.

Steinberg   USA

BOMM !...

Tan   Turkey

Sabuncu   Turkey

East versus West

At the centre of the arms race is an ideological conflict between "the East" and "the West". This conflict manifests itself in many ways not least of all in nuclear capability and in support for one side or the other in many recent wars.

The cartoons on the next few pages are all about this East-West conflict, they could be usefully supplemented by others, for example those on pages 26-27.

It may be useful to ask people to brainstorm about the idea of East-West conflict before looking at the cartoons. Then review the cartoons - what do they suggest about the nature of the conflict?

- How do these ideas compare with the original list?

- What are the consequences of the East-West conflict?

Oliphant   USA

Brigitte Schneider   Germany

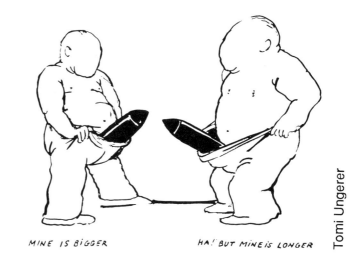

MINE IS BIGGER   HA! BUT MINE IS LONGER

Tomi Ungerer

DROITS DE L'HOMME

Plantu   France

ANOTHER IDENTITY CRISIS

'OUT OF THE WAY, YOU COMMIE NUISANCE — ER, NOT YOU, LEONID... THIS OTHER GUY!'

Oliphant   USA

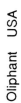

NUCLEAR WEAPONS IN THE PACIFIC

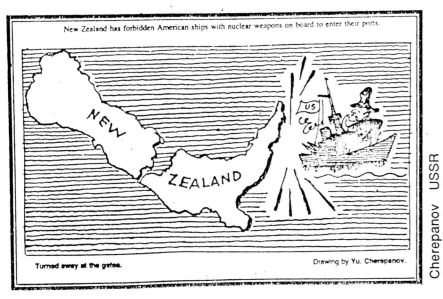

Cherepanov USSR

Austin Britain

In peace time?

Since World War II the level of violence has heightened. There are more local and regional conflicts and more people killed by them. Excluding the two world wars, 83 wars started before 1945, 120 since then; four times as many deaths have occurred since World War II than before it. These years have seen a significant increase in civil conflicts.

The location as well as the nature of war is changing. Since 1945 wars have been fought almost exclusively in the Third World. With the heavy flow of advanced weaponry from the industrialized to the poorer countries, no hamlet, no matter how remote, is far from the battlefield. Death rates in wars are poorly recorded. Where fatality rates are available for both civilians and soldiers, civilian deaths are sharply higher. Wars are now more life-threatening for non-combatants than for the people fighting them.

Of the 203 conflicts this century so far :

- 33 have occurred in Latin America

- 29 have occurred in Europe

- 22 have occurred in The Middle East

- 19 have occurred in Southern Asia

- 54 have occurred in the Far East

- 31 have occurred in Sub-Saharan Africa

- 15 have occurred in other parts of Africa

Estimated total number of deaths = 78 million

Source: Sivard, R. Leger [1985] World Military and Social Expenditures, Washington.

Claudius Switzerland

Disarm!

As we go to press, another round of disarmament talks are taking place in Geneva. They look like they might have some real results, but will they fundamentally change anything?

The cartoons on these two pages could be used as a stimulus to discuss how people see the disarmament talks.

Boycott

The 1980 Olympic Games were held in Moscow; they were boycotted by the USA. The cartoons on pages 80-81 were all drawn in the USA at that time.

• What are these cartoons saying about why the USA boycotted the games?

The 1984 Olympic Games were held in Los Angeles .... they were boycotted by the USSR.

• Did they have similar justification?

MacNelly USA

Moir Australia

Rozantsev USSR

Martyn Turner Ireland

John Thornton USA

SOVIET 'OLYMPICS'

Ed Fischer USA

Eric Smith USA

Craig Macintosh USA

MOSCOW OLYMPICS

WAR CRIMES AGAINST AFGHAN CIVILIANS

Charles Werner USA

OLYMPIC COVERAGE

HEAR NO EVIL

SEE NO EVIL

SPEAK NO EVIL

1980

CHUCK AYERS

© 1980 AKRON BEACON JOURNAL

Chuck Ayers USA

BOYCOTT THE OLYMPICS

U.S. AID

FROM: WHITE HOUSE
TO: AFGHANISTAN

Horsey USA

A world of doves

We have found cartoons from all over the world which feature the dove as a symbol of peace. The next few pages are a small collection of them.

They could be used in a number of ways as stimulus for discussion about peace. Like the globe cartoons on pages 36-41, they provide a good starting point for an activity to draw a cartoon.

Naji al Ali   Lebanon

Yayo   Colombia

Olivier Raynaud   France

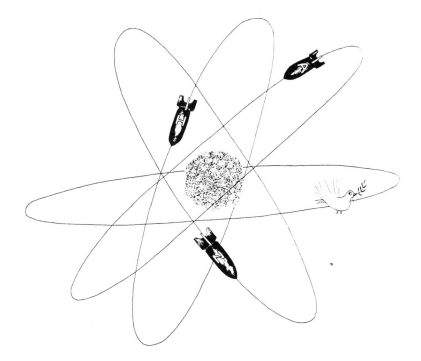

Lillo Cuba

Hankour Algeria

J. Arce Bolivia

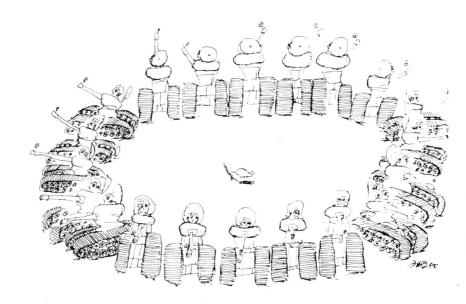

Jeno Dallos Hungary

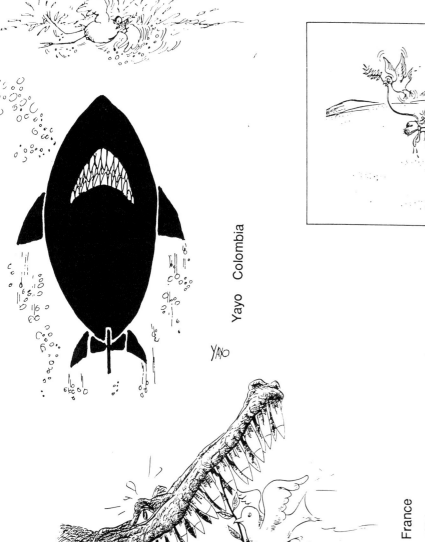

Yayo Colombia

YAYO

MIDDLE EAST

'84 L.C.C.

J. F. Batellier France

JF. Batellier
3/84

To read

Common Security: A Programme for Disarmament [Independent Commission on Disarmament and Security Issues (The Palme Commission), Pan, 1982.]
Introductory but comprehensive review of the links between disarmament, peace and development.

World Military and Social Expenditures [Ruth Sivard, World Priorities, USA (yearly).]
Detailed review of military spending, arms build up and world military strength.

The Arms Bazaar [Sampson, A., Hodder & Stoughton, 1977.]
Expose of the arms industry, who benefits, who loses?

Diary for a Habitable Planet [E.P. Thompson and D. Smith (eds), Penguin, 1987.]
Excellent collection of essays examining East/West and North South dimensions of the arms crisis.

For Teaching

Peace [Chris Sewell, Spokesman, 1987.]
Excellent "easyreader" on peace - includes many case studies e.g. Einstein, Martin Luther King, Ghandi etc.

A Manual on Non Violence and Children [Stephanie Judson (ed), New Society publishers, 1984 (originally 1977).]
A manual of information and co-operative games for children and adults.

"Human Rights are as old as human society itself, for they derive from every person's need to realise their essential humanity. They are not ephemeral, not alterable with time and place and circumstance. They are not the problem of philosophical whim or political fashion. They have their origin in the fact of the human condition; and because they have, they are fundamental and inalienable. More specifically, they are not conferred by constitutions, conventions or governments ..... they were born not of man, but with man".

- Shridath Ramphal.

In the Western world when reference is made to human rights, most of us think in terms of civil or political rights. The right to vote, the right to free assembly, to free speech. However, for many people around the world these rights often appear secondary alongside a more fundamental human right - survival. Current economic and political situations deny them that right. Organisations such as Amnesty International document tens of thousands of cases of illegal detention, torture and assassination.

Following the devastation of the second world war, the United Nations attempted to give clear expression and effect to human rights through the 1948 Universal Declaration of Human Rights. The Declaration contains over 30 articles each one covering a particular human right.

The Declaration states that everyone has a right to:

- Life, liberty and security of person.
- Food, clothing, housing, an adequate standard of living.
- Work, rest, health, education.
- Form trade unions , enjoy the benefits of cultural life and science.
- Freedom of thought, conscience and religion.
- Equal treatment in the courts.
- Be presumed innocent until proven guilty.
- Peaceful assembly.
- Freedom of association.
- Take part in public affairs.

Anyone deprived of liberty shall be treated with humanity. No one shall be subject to: -torture, slavery, forced labour or arbitrary interference with their privacy, family, home or correspondence.

The UN Declaration has been criticised for placing too much emphasis on individual rights while neglecting community rights; for paying scant attention to economic and social rights while highlighting political rights and for not emphasising the duties which accompany the demand for rights. Whatever its shortcomings the UN Declaration provides the only agreed code for recognising human rights.

The reality of poverty and inequality throughout the world testifies to the fact that peoples' economic rights are ignored and violated. The Third World today contains 75% of the world's people but has only 17% of world GNP, 15% of energy consumption, 30% of food grains, 18% of export earnings, 11% of world education spending, 6% of health expenditure, 50% of science and technology and 8% of industry. And the situation is not getting better ..... In the developed world, the growing influence of monetarism in time of recession ensures a life of poverty for millions and a life of riches for a few.

The annual Amnesty International Report shows a systematic abuse of political and social human rights. Throughout the world, in Europe, the United States, the Soviet Union and beyond, human rights are violated daily. These violations are conducted in the name of "freedom", "peace" and "democracy". From Afghanistan to Nicaragua to El Salvador, Chile and Iran, Northern Ireland, Britain and India, governments claim to uphold human rights while vigorously denying them at the same time. They justify their own actions with reference to the equally unjust actions of their opponents.

There is however another side to the coin. Over the past few decades human rights violations have become the focus of widespread international activism. There can be little doubt that the existence of organisations such as Amnesty has helped create a climate where abuses become more difficult. It is through the constant publicising of rights violations that pressure can be brought to bear.

The need for and strength of the human rights movement is both a condemnation of and a hope for the contemporary world. It is sad that ordinary citizens have to force their governments to respect human rights and it is a source of inspiration and hope, especially for those suffering, that they continue to do so.

The main theme of this section is human rights. It starts by using a small collection of cartoons to ask the question - what do we mean human rights? We then review this question in the context of the UN Declaration of Human Rights.

Cartoonists can often be in the frontline of political comment and find themselves a focus for a backlash which violates these human rights. We have outlined some examples.

This section is completed by a collection of cartoons which focus on South Africa and apartheid.

Human Rights: what do we mean?

Select a set of cartoons and give them to each pair in the group. Ask them to rank them in terms of those they feel raise the most important issues about human rights. Suggest that they use a diamond shape, placing those they think raise the most important issues at the top and those they think least important at the bottom.

Give plenty of time for pairs to reach their concensus about an order. This process will not only provide a focus for the group discussion but also mean that everyone will be more prepared to join in having aired their ideas in small groups.

A recent Development Education Centre publication; **'Do it justice!'** is about human rights education, it stresses the need to start by seeing human rights in the context of our own society rather than always, like the man in the cartoon on page 95, focusing on violations in other parts of the world.

Claudius Switzerland

"Oh, yes, I adore Amnesty – that is the one with Blake Carrington, right?"

Taylor Britain

Mike Peters USA

Claudius Switzerland

Evans   Britain

4/75 J.F.Batellier.   J. F. Batellier   France

Kodjo Crobsen   Ghana

"IT WAS ALL NKRUMAH'S FAULT. IF HE HADN'T SENT SO MANY TO SCHOOL THERE WOULDN'T HAVE BEEN SO MANY USELESS ARGUMENTS TODAY"

Fran   Kenya

"I've no wish to take the chairperson's job. But since you ask for frankness, I must say I do not feel comfortable about being her deputy!"

The United Nations Declaration

In 1948 the United Nations signed the **Universal Declaration of Human Rights** which laid out an agreed set of rights for all people in all nations. The Declaration came just after World War II when there was a world wide desire for peace and justice. It was hoped that by respecting each person and their basic needs, the world would be a better and fairer place.

The Declaration is seen by many people to be "a common standard of achievement". It says that human dignity and equality are things we should try to achieve. It says that all people are equal regardless of "race, colour, sex, language, religion, political or other opinion, national or social origin, property, birth or other status".

Human Rights mean human responsibilities as well. If we want something for ourselves then we have a duty to see that others have it also.

Understanding, tolerance and friendship are just a few of the keywords in the Declaration.

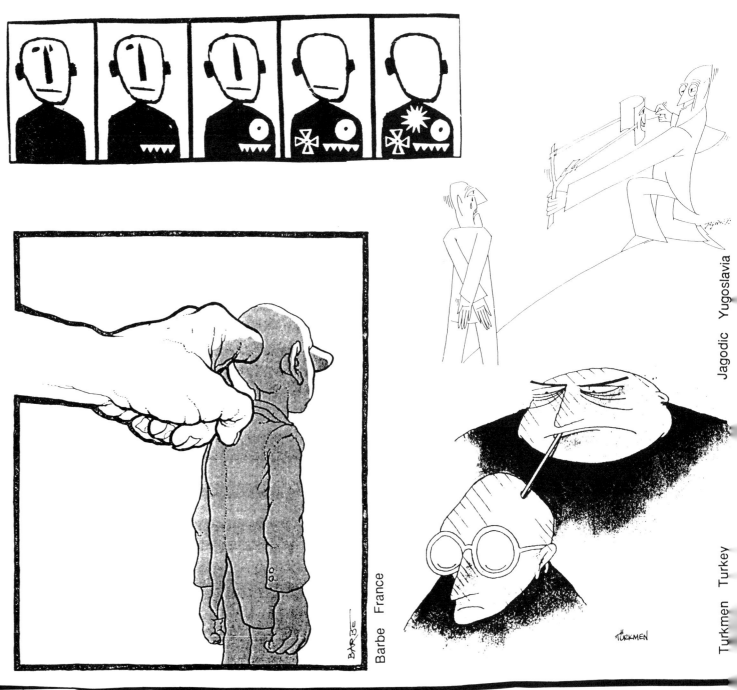

Jagodic Yugoslavia

Barbe France

Turkmen Turkey

Coplu Turkey

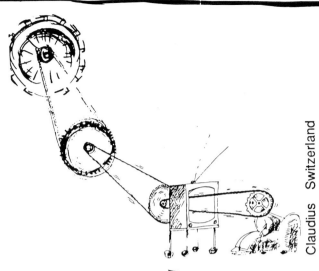

Claudius Switzerland

7 footnotes to **SELF-CENSORSHIP***

* It is in the interest of national security.
  * I trust our leaders.
    * I need to retain friends in high places.
      * I need this job.
        * I need a promotion.
          * I need to stay out of jail.
            * Anyhow the other side is worse.

Feiffer USA

Martyn Turner Ireland

Naji al Ali Lebanon

Some basic Human Rights

No-one shall be subjected to arbitrary arrest, detention or exile.

Everyone has the right to freedom of thought, conscience and religion.

Everyone has the right to life, liberty and the security of person.

Everyone has the right to freedom of opinion and expression.

No-one shall be subjected to torture or to cruel, inhuman or degrading treatment or punishment.

Everyone has the right to work, to free choice of employment, to just and favourable conditions of work and to protection against unemployment.

Everyone has the right to a nationality.

Everyone has the right of education.

Everyone has the right to own property alone as well as in association with others.

Everyone is entitled to a social and international order in which the rights and freedoms set forth in this declaration can be fully realised.

'My people! The hated dictatorship is over! From now on, you will elect me democratically!'

..THAT'S FINE : I'M READY TO KILL FOR MINE!

..I AM READY TO DIE FOR MY BELIEFS!

J. F. Batellier   France

Zloczower

SQUIB

You must not judge us too harshly minister! We are not all corrupt little tin-pot governments!

Why, only recently we brought in a new package of reforms!

?

For example, land reform! If the people demand land we make sure they get their own individual plot!!!

Ah yes... six feet by two!!!

© Pete Vujakovic 1986

Pete Vujakovic   Britain

I'M IN FOR A MASS MURDER, AND YOU?

TRYING TO PREVENT ONE!

S. Roth   Australia

LONDON AIRPORT CUSTOMS

WE'VE BEEN PROTESTING AGAINST THE PINOCHET REGIME — IT ISN'T FASCIST ENOUGH!

CHILE MATCH   British airways

Hector Breeze   Britain

NEED A LIGHT PAL?

© Francis Boyle

NICARAGUA   CONTRAS

STATUE OF HYPOCRISY

GIVE ME YOUR TIRED, YOUR POOR DICTATORS, YOUR HUDDLED FASCISTS

Francis Boyle   Britain

Don Wright USA

"I don't know about you, but I couldn't half pacify a cold lager...."

Bill Stott Britain

S. Kneebone Australia

Claudius Switzerland

Claudius Switzerland

Cork Holland

Tomas Cnoff

"It's a pity Martin Luther King couldn't have preached the brotherhood of man like you do without stirring people up."

Bruce Petty Australia

Plantu France

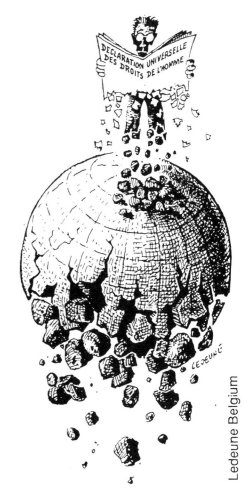

Ledeune Belgium

Choe Vietnam

Cartoonists have rights too!

"The political cartoon has been one of the most powerful weapons through the ages. ..... Dictators of the right and the left fear the political cartoonist . ... No totalitarian government can afford to be ridiculed."

Art Buckwalk, Cartoons for Amnesty

This fear of cartoons has led to many cases of cartoonists losing their rights.

In Uruguay cartoonist Francisco Laurenzo Pons was in jail for nearly ten yeas with no charges specified. Amnesty International designated him a 'prisoner of conscience' which led to international lobbies for his release.

In China recent changes have allowed cartoonists to play their role in the political scene. They can now caricature the country's leaders..as long as they do it "respectfully". In 1942, Mao Tse-tung laid down the dictum, adopted from the Soviets, that revolutionary figures must receive wholly positive artistic treatment.

In Turkey recent years have seen an increasing number of journalists jailed for their work because it is seen to be against article 42 of their penal code which prohibits "making communist propaganda". Recently Prime Minister Turgut Ozal complained about the way he was lampooned in satirical cartoons - which led to cases against an editor and three cartoonists.

In Vietnam Choe [Nguyen Hai Chi], who drew the cartoons on this page, was arrested as a "communist agent" by the Thieu government. Later he was arrested as a "reactionary counterrevolutionary element" by the Communist government and sent to a "re-education camp".

Naji al-Ali

During the final stages of putting this book together the Lebanese cartoonist Naji al-Ali was shot in London. He died in September 1987.

"From Lebanon to Kuwait, the cartoonist has so far survived attempts to stop his work". So wrote Index on Censorship in 1984. The article identified strict censorship of the written word in many Middle East countries and the high illiteracy rates as major factors in the influence of cartoons. They are one of the few outlets for political criticism.

Naji al-Ali first started to draw cartoons on the walls of his camp in the 1950's at a time when there was a growing political awareness among refugees. He felt that the political cartoonist should provide a new vision. This role, as he saw it, meant criticizing corruption and double standards wherever he saw them rather than taking the side of a particular political group.

He had Hanzala, the child who appears in all his cartoons, to help him. He described Hanzala, who always has his hands behind his back as a symbol of rejection of many negative tides, as "an icon to watch me from slipping".

Index on Censorship asked him - Does the continuous deterioration of civil liberties in the Middle East give you a sense of despair? - he responded. .... "When I was younger I thought I would actually be able to help achieve all our aspirations for independence, unity, justice. Many died for those aspirations and things are only getting worse. That, certainly, can make one despair. But, more than ever, I feel a sense of duty to go on doing what I have to do and can do."

Naji al Ali Lebanon

"Butrus is a Christian Copt - he's been charged with belonging to an underground organisation. After torture he was made to say he belonged to the 'Muslim Brotherhood'."

Naji al Ali   Lebanon

Naji al Ali   Lebanon

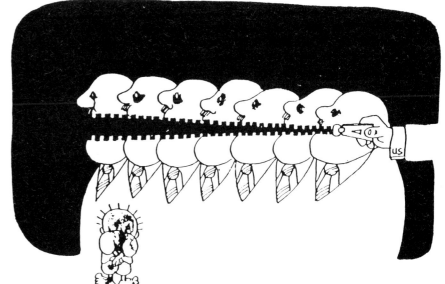

Naji al Ali   Lebanon

Further examples of Naji al-Ali's work are to be found on pages, 4,9,49,5l, 82 and 9l.

Human rights in South Africa

The next few pages focus on human rights in South Africa, the apartheid system and our involvement in it. Cartoons such as these provide a valuable stimulus for opening up discussion about the issues involved. In particular cartoons of this type help unpack some of the complex arguments presented to mask what is clearly a massive basic injustice.

We introduce the section by reproducing part of an interview from Target Magazine in which Jock Leyden, a South African cartoonist talks about apartheid.

How long have you been dealing with the issue of apartheid as a professional cartoonist living in South Africa?

Since I started doing political cartoons for the Sunday and Daily Tribunes in 1937. My paper has opposed the Nationalist Party [the party advocating apartheid] and its policies ever since it came to power in 1948. Unremitting opposition, I might add!

Before the South African government imposed the current press restrictions on coverage of violent demonstrations, what other government restrictions did South African journalists labour under?

The Defence [Military] Act, the Police Act, and the Prisons Act make reporting of affairs connected with these three branches something to approach with care. Photographing and drawing in areas connected with them is forbidden.

There's none so blind . . .

"It's the latest thing in riot gear, mate."

Does the South African press reflect the spectrum of opinions regarding apartheid policy?

Not really. All the English-language newspapers have opposed the policy of apartheid - and have never let up in their opposition and call for its complete abolition. Many people outside South Africa do not seem to be even remotely aware of this.

What is your working relationship with your editor?

I have always had a free hand in my work. But I would never - no matter the salary offered - work for any paper with whose editorial policy I did not agree! Naturally, the editor must okay my cartoons before publication. It is he who is responsible for what appears in the newspaper and must take the rap if there is any backlash. But my editor is an outspoken critic of apartheid policies in all forms.

Have the South African political cartoonists ever gotten together to discuss the apartheid issue?

The only time I have ever met all of South Africa's cartoonists was in 1981 when I went to Johannesburg to receive the "Cartoonist of the Year" award. We don't need to get together to discuss apartheid. It is obvious from the cartoons we do that we all abhor it. It's amazing just how hard-hitting many of them are. Lots of people might wonder how we get away with it. '

The cartoons in this collection could be used as an introduction to the issue and to enable groups to share their attitudes and assumptions. They can also be used to build up an agenda of things they need to study in greater depth.

It would also be important to give time to discussion about our involvement in South Africa and what the group feel should be done about it.

In 1984 the Carngie Corporation published the results of a major study of poverty and apartheid. The report gives a detailed account at macro and micro levels of the current position in South Africa, analysing the long-term trends and the causes of poverty among blacks.

The findings, backed by thorough academic inquiry, shatter three widely-held myths.

The myths

1. That however deprived in political and civil rights terms, black South Africans are relatively well off in economic terms compared with blacks in other African countries;

2. That while some blacks still live in poverty in South Africa, the trend is towards a rising standard of living;

3. That South Africa's poverty, illiteracy and disease levels are attributable to general under-development in the context of a Third World continent.

Martyn Turner   Ireland

The real story

The report shows these statements to be untrue and instead provides a detailed analysis of the statistics of poverty and apartheid.

Nearly nine million blacks currently live below the minimum subsistence level in the home-lands. The number has doubled in the past 20 years, and the number of people living in the homelands without any income stood at 1.43 million in 1980, compared with a quarter of a million in 1960.

The findings established also that this level of poverty is a direct result, not of poor resources, drought or historical accident, but of apartheid policies.

Education, skills training and stable employ-ment are the privilege of the relatively few, and it is these few who are seen by visitors to South Africa.

Those blacks who by accident of birth and the good fortune of continuous employment have established tenuous legal rights in the cities have been able to improve their standards of living in the past 20 years. Most of them still live close to the poverty line in overcrowded, inse-cure townships, but as a relatively privileged group they are a diminishing proportion of blacks in South Africa.

....

Plantu France

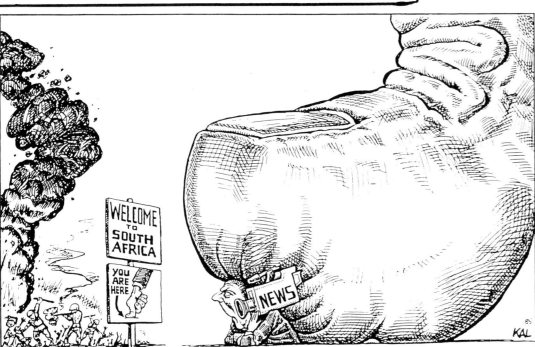

Kal Britain

FAIR FIGHT

Grayston Canada

The Sowetan   South Africa

Mike Lane

Wasserman   USA

South African society is based on a system of social engineering reaching into the lives of its citizens. Wealth, income and ownership are concentrated heavily in the hands of the white minority. The process began with white seizure of 85% of the land, and was reinforced as first the mines and then industry were developed under white control. Africans, who comprise more than 70% of the population, received in 1980 just 29% of all personal income. They must live apart from whites, in townships designed to be easily sealed off by the army.

Apartheid's essential feature is the control of black labour through restrictive legislation and the concentration of huge numbers of blacks in areas designated as homelands, independent states, or derisively, 'bantustans'. No less than three and a half million people were moved between 1960 and 1982 in order to implement the model. The Churches have taken a lead in condemning this programme of relocations.

The inevitable consequence is desperate poverty in the bantustans. Even in relatively well-off Bophutatswana, three-fifths of the population earn less than the bare minimum household subsistence level. The bantustans are rural slums rather than farming areas. Over half their population is unemployed, and over three quarters of bantustan income is from migrant labour in white South Africa. Inflation erodes what people can buy. The consequences are malnutrition, disease and death. 55% of all African deaths in South Africa are children under the age of five, compared to just 7% for whites.

Steve Bell   Britain

Gibbard   Britain

Auth   USA

Gibbard   Britain

MAGGIE TAKES A STANCE ON APARTHEID —

Cummings Canada

Borg

Bas Greece

To read

Bread and Freedom
[Ron O'Grady, World Cnl of Churches, 1981]
Very readable introduction to human rights and their relationship to everyday life.

Against Oblivion
[Jonathan Power, Fontana, 1981.]
The story of Amnesty International.

The Apartheid Handbook
[Roger Omond, Pelican, 1986, 1st 1985]
Readable and detailed review of the mechanics of racism in South Africa.

Biko
[Donald Woods, Penguin, 1986, 1st 1978]
The story of just one of the opponents of apartheid and the price he paid for it.

For Teaching

Teaching and Learning about Human Rights [Amnesty Int. British Section, 1986.]
Pack of 11 units dealing with the UN Charter, Rights, Prisoners of Conscience, Torture etc. with suggested teaching activities.

Do it justice - activities and resources
[Development Ed. Centre, B'ham 1988]
A book to introduce teaching activities. and over one hundred teaching resources which can be adapted to work on human rights.

Profile on Prejudice
[Nikki van der Gaag and Lynne Gerlach, Minority Rights Group, 1985.]
Teaching pack focussing on the rights of minorities - includes case studies of Travellers, Palestinians and Native Americans.

We live in a world of generalisations, we said, generalising. We couldn't write, speak or cartoon without them. At its mildest the stereotype is a simple visual generalisation representing a group, country or type. At its worst it is a deliberately manipulated tool of propaganda. Like most generalisations you can see it for what it is and accept or question it as you wish. To a cartoonist the stereotypes are vital, s/he could hardly work without them.

The official stereotype has considerable potential. John Bull and Uncle Sam are terrific images which can be used as direct representations or manipulated as desired. They seem as popular with friends as with enemies. While working in Japan for a year Ranan Lurie, the American cartoonist, created an image for Japan which was accepted on behalf of the nation by the Prime Minister. The following year Lurie was commissioned to create a similar character for Taiwan and the South China Post ran a lucrative competition for cartoonists who managed to incorporate this character into a cartoon.

Nobody, we hope, actually believes that the average Englishman looks like John Bull or that the average Englishman is a thin bowler hatted pin striped, nose in the air chap you may see in a cartoon. But what is the poor cartoonist to do? Faced with the task of drawing representatives of the member nations of the EEC they either have to draw twelve people in grey suits marked Frenchman, Spaniard, etc. or resort to stereotypes. It is a visual shorthand that means Frenchmen wear berets and prisoners always have arrows or stripes on their suits.

On a more harmful level is the creation of a false stereotype which through repetition takes on a truth of its own. One only has to watch an American film on Russia to wonder why the nation of militaristic monsters who live somewhere to the east of us have been so singularily unsuccessful in their avowed aim of dominating the world. The popular film image of Russians in America is reinforced by the cartoonists. One of them always draws Russian soldiers as rhinoceroses, an effect which fails to achieve its purpose as he draws them "kinda cute".

The Russians respond in kind. Graphically, Russians are always smooth faced and cherubic and Americans look like refugee Nazis from British war comics. They have three days growth of beard, slitty eyes and festering eyebrows.

Stereotypes can be both unfair and dangerous but stereotyping seems inevitable and can never be obliterated. The human beast is a herd animal, we join groups and swear allegiance at the drop of a hat and without the slightest concern for logic or fact.

The Chelsea supporter who believes with religious fervour that Chelsea are gods to a man and Arsenal are pre reptilian underbeings will continue to believe that even if the entire Arsenal team was transferred to Chelsea and vice versa.

Development Education is about internationalism, it has a role to play in challenging nationalism, when it takes on a narrow or xenophobic outlook not unlike these Chelsea/Arsenal supporters. Development Education has a role in challenging stereotypes as a basis for thinking, but we also have to beware that we do not simply offer another allegiance to swear, another group to join, new stereotypes and new non-thinking to adopt. It is so tempting to think that these are the limitations of groups on "the right" and that such does not go on in "the centre" or on "the left". We tend not to see our own stereotypes or at least, if we do we see them, we see them as acceptable.

It is all too easy, for example in the name of "enlightened thinking" to manage information in an attempt to create new stereotypes which are "more positive". The need for positive images to balance the dominant view of marginalised groups and other countries is clear. The danger is however, that in doing this we run the risk of making a new packaged off pat analysis and end up limiting our ability to question what is going on or what could be done about it.

In this section we consider the role of stereotypes in cartoons and how stereotypes influence our thinking. We use a collection about the Falklands and cartoons by Jak and Cormac to explore the role of cartoons in the processes of "dehumanising the enemy". We invite you use cartoons as a stimulus for discussing how you see the relationship between Britain and Ireland. The section is completed with a collection of cartoons to question whether or not we all have our own acceptable stereotypes.

75 : 25
- a cartoon to challenge or reinforce?

This cartoon was drawn as an illustration for a book with the title '**75 : 25 Ireland in an unequal world**' It was published by CON-GOOD which is a network which brings together organisations which are trying to raise an awareness of world injustice.

The idea of the cartoon was to show that 25% of the world's people use some 83% of its wealth and that 75% of the people have to make do with 17% of it! This cartoon received a number of quite different reactions, in particular about its "use of stereotypes". Some for example thought it was not a cartoon worthy of use in a development education book. What do you think?

It may be helpful to point out features such as, the shape of the globe, the thin capitalist and his ability to out weigh all the others and the expressions on their faces.
In contrast the Brazilian poster makes use of the symbol of a fat capitalist as the key feature in the cartoon. The caption reads ....

".. and are you going to tighten your belt too?"
"No thank you I use braces!"

• Do you think this is a good use of stereotypes?

• Is your reaction different to the 75:25 one?

• If so why do you think that is so?

The poster was produced by a Brazilian group called Nucleo de Educacao Popular [Grass root Education Group] who are working to increase awareness among the people of Sao Paulo. Like the group in Ireland they are raising questions about injustice.

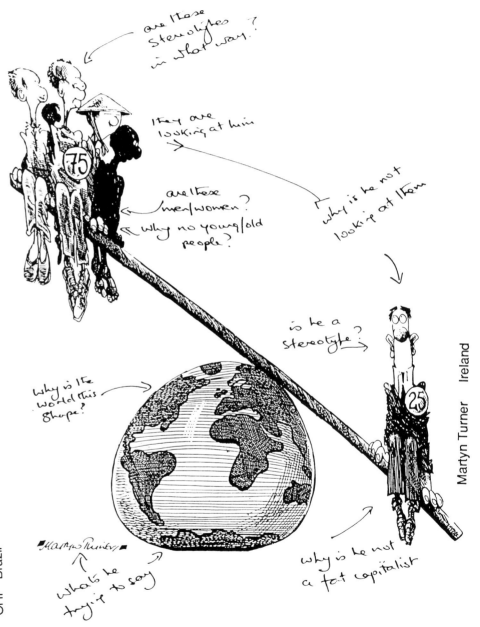

Teagues, Prods, Brits, Huns, Nips, Jocks, Yanks, Ruskies, Taffies and Chinks

by **Harry Barton**

Someone told me a policeman had complained that I'd idealised an IRA man in a play I'd written. I felt sad. I've liked policemen ever since a day in the years before television when Dick Barton, Special Agent, was a name on radio. My seven-year-old son and I had occasion to visit a London police station. I gave our name, which even then was Barton. The sergeant leaned over the counter and addressed the small boy. "And which one of you", he asked "is Dick".

So I think I'd like to try to explain. I have no desire to idealise an IRA man, or any of his equivalents, orange or green. I'd rather idealise a bad potato: all it can ever do to you is make a smell.

But I don't stereotype either - or I try not to: and I suspect this policeman was a stereotyper. It's what we do to our opponents, particularly if we've let them get to be the kind of opponents who will kill us if we don't kill them. It's easier to kill a stereotype than a human being. So we stereotype each other. We call each other Teagues, Prods, Brits, Huns, Nips, Jocks, Yanks, Russkies, Taffies and Chinks.

When the Falklands started, there had to be Argies. Once we had the Argies, the barbarians felt free to yell "Gotcha!" when an Argentinian ship was torpedoed and hundreds drowned. Argies were not people.

The terrorist in my play is a person, not a stereotype. I made him one of the intelligent ones because they pose the interesting puzzle. They live in these islands, one of the few places where humanity has begun to develop a little freedom of speech and movement, a little stability and justice. Most other places on earth have governments that are themselves terrorist organisations. Wouldn't our terrorists feel more at home in one of those places - Russia, say, or South Africa, or El Salvador? Wouldn't they feel more useful?

Miss Bernadette Devlin, as she then was, published her book. The Price of My Soul, in 1969. I'd been away for thirty years and it helped me to get back into the island. I warmed to the book. I reviewed it on 'What's West', in one of the earliest editions of that ancient programme, broad-casting live from a bedroom on the second floor of the old Melville Hotel. I said, pompously but honestly, that I thought Bernadette would be a great Irishwomen if she grew up to be non-violent. Which, I often think, she nearly did. But she allowed the provocations to be too much for her. the injustices; the poverty in Cookstown; the Paisleyites at Burntollet; the horrid muddle and loose paving stones of Derry. She reverted to tribalism. She stereotyped her opponents, and they stereotyped her, and bullets eventually damaged her.

But she's not a stereotype; she's a human being whom we elected to parliament.

Now, there's Gerry Adams, M.P. He looks like an amateur actor made up for the part of a 1960's university lecturer, his subject probably social administration. He seems on television to have two traits of the power-monger, he smiles to himself, as though relishing his power, and when faced with that awkward thing, a civilised question, he sinks smoothly into standard gobbledygook. He's another product of deprivation, another person elected on a straight tribal vote, another man who's prepared to stereotype his opponents and see them killed.

It's tempting to stereotype violent people. But they are human beings and there's no doubt we'll cope with them better if we understand this. They make stereotypes of the rest of us. Otherwise they might not be able to bring themselves to use armalities on us as well as ballot papers. But that doesn't mean that we should stereotype them. If we do, then I think we'll find we've joined them. Myself, I'd rather eat a bad potato.

Dehumanising the enemy

- "GOTCHA"

If you pick up many children's comics you could get the impression that World War II rages on. More recently the Falklands have provided another opportunity for romanticising war and showing the stupidity of the enemy.

A brief visit to the newsagent can provide a considerable source of such stimulus material to discuss this sort of imagery and how it may influence the attitudes of young people.

At the time of the Falklands war the coverage in a number of popular British newspapers reduced the situation to a similar level. The Sun, which the Gibbard cartoon suggests, was perhaps the most obvious, published the article on the page opposite which captures something of the attitudes which soon grew up.

A number of the cartoons at the time lent strength to the notion that Argentina could be no match at all for Britain. In fact "laughing with Clive Collins" in the Sun is so crude that it even looks like propaganda. Çummings [see page 115] suggests that any questioning about what was going on was unpatriotic. This kind of attitude to Mrs Thatcher was very significant in the build up to, and eventual outcome of the 1983 election.

The cartoons on the next few pages were all drawn at the time of the Falklands / Malvinas war. They could be used to explore the issues involved and to introduce factors such as the interest of the arms industry or the role of the war in terms of domestic politics in both Britain and Argentina.

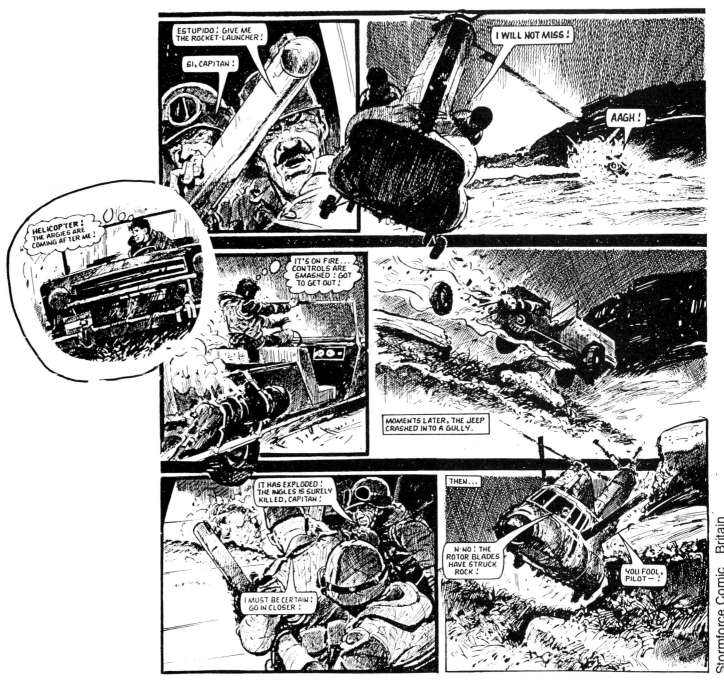

Stormforce Comic   Britain

ARGY BARGY BLITZ!

The jokes are flooding in

Ever since The Sun's Argy Bargie jokes first appeared, your very own gags have been pouring in. They are so funny that we have decided to give £5 for every reader's Argy-Bargie joke published. Plus a can of Fray Bentos "non-Argentinian" corn beef.

Today's joke was told to us by Titus Rowlandson, 9, from Brighton. This is it:

'A lone Royal Marine stands on the top of a hill on the Falklands, laughing and jeering at the Argentine troops below.

This so angers the Argentine general that he sends 10 of his best men to deal with him. After an almighty row, everything goes quiet and the Marine reappears still laughing and jeering.

The general sends 100 men over the top. The same thing happens.

The general is so furious that he sends 1000 of his men to deal with the marine. When they're half way-up the hill, they are met by a lone wounded Argentine survivor. With his last breath he whispers to them: "Go back, go back! It's a trap. There's two of them!'

From The Sun

You understand I will not hesitate to defend my political career to the last man...

Si, señora — we of the junta feel the same way!

Great — a basis for understanding

Oliphant USA

Gibbard Britain

I hereby claim these islands in the name of anti-colonialism!

Auth USA

from Peru

It's a hectic bank holiday in the Falkland Islands:

'Ere Larry — d'you wanna know something really amazing?

Yeah? Whassat?

Did you know the British Army is actually importing mutton into this place?

Well you could knock me down with a feather, Laz — that's a real mind boggler!!

I call it a disgrace — if we're worth dying for we must be worth eating!!

Yeah?

© Steve Bell 1984

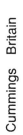

PATRIOTISM

"Shocking! Someone's written a dirty word!"

Cummings

Cummings Britain

COMING HOME TO ROOST

Garland Britain

DONATO
TORONTO SUN

Donato Canada

Cartoons 'n conflict

Jak and Cormac are both noted for commenting on Northern Ireland. Cormac has a regular weekly strip in An Phoblacht [Republican News]. Jak publishes in a number of British "popular" papers.

The cartoon here is drawn by Jak for the Evening Standard in London. It has become quite famous. It inspired groups in England to organise demonstrations, write letters and to shape their ideas in a book about the media treatment of the Irish in Britain called **'Nothing but the same old story'**.

The GLC [Greater London Council] decided to withdraw an advertising budget worth some £100,000 from the Standard. Ken Livingstone the leader of the GLC said

"the clear message of the cartoon is that the Irish as a race and as a community , are murderous, mindless thugs ...... I do not believe in free speech for racists ... We will not put another penny into the Standard while it continues to vilify the Irish."

But the cartoon in question was one of Jak's better efforts. Drawn soon after the bomb at the Conservative party conference hotel in Brighton, it reflected the general opinion, at that time, that many British people felt about the Irish. No one was suggesting that every Irishman was a terrorist but they may well have felt that if the terrorists were such a minute percentage of the population at large how come they held such sway over the population for such a long time.

Cormac   Ireland

Cormac   Ireland

Yet in other cartoons by Jak he displays an over eagerness to add to the "thick paddy" stereotype. The Irish Army has served in the U.N. Peace-keeping force in the Lebanon for a number of years. Quite a number have died, trying to keep different factions from each others throats. Yet in a cartoon about the Lebanon he is eager to show us what he thinks of the Irish by drawing their shamrock and label upside down. It is gratuitous, having nothing to do with the message of the cartoon. In a similar way he adds an incidental notice about "Thick Irish Sausages", in a cartoon which shows tourists in London.

Likewise, Cormac pushes a line, which, as it says in the introduction to a recent collection of his cartoons, is rarely seen in the British media. Are his cartoons designed to challenge or simply to back up an "anti-Brit" viewpoint already assumed to be held by his readership? This role gives the cartoonist an active role in the process "dehumanising of the enemy". [See page 112]

Danny Morrison, writing as editor of An Phoblacht, says of Cormac ...

"In his cartoons he belittles the enemy and boosts the morale of the oppressed, and his acerbic, supportive comments, particularly on the IRA operations, have outraged The Guardian and the editor of the Irish Press. The rest of us, however, have been entertained."

Both cartoonists are, we think, trivialising a complex reality and dehumanising the real situation. They encourage their very different readerships not to see those involved as people. They do not help us to question the issues involved, they ask only that we adopt their stereotype.

Going further.... how do you see it?

The collection of cartoons on the next few pages are all about the relationship between Britain and Ireland. The three of us who put **'Thin Black Lines'** together live on either side of "the water", so it is natural that the relationship between the two countries should come to mind,

Our concern about international issues and development has taught us that there is much to learn from this our local "international relationship". This idea is taken much further in **'Half the lies are true - Britain and Ireland as a microcosm of international misunderstanding'**. [See page 129]

A very fruitful stimulus to discussion is to be found in using cartoons such as these. Provide each group with a selection. Ask them to identify the issues which are, for them, raised by each of the cartoons. Then ask them to rank them in order of how important that issue is to the relationship between Britain and Ireland.

It is important to bear in mind that, more than the cartoons, it is the groups perceptions which are providing the material for the discussion.

The process of putting **'Thin Back Lines'** together has provided us with many opportunities for reflection and for looking at things sideways. It seems to us that many, in both Britain and Ireland, find it easier to become outraged by what is happening in Central America or South Africa than on our own doorstep. On the other hand we also find that many people concerned about issues of justice and human rights at home are content to reduce justice to charity when it occurs on a world stage. We all have our blind spots ..... we all have our stereotypes.

Martyn Turner   Ireland

Martyn Turner   Ireland

THERE WERE THESE THICK PADDIES........

Starrett

Phil Evans

Evans Britain

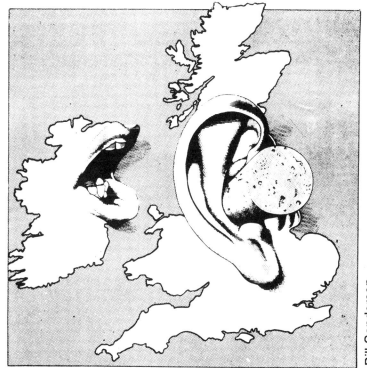

Bill Sanderson

Martyn Turner   Ireland

Martyn Turner   Ireland

Martyn Turner   Ireland

Kal   Britain

"The only solution to the Irish problem is to understand that no solution works"

Cummings Britain

Pete Wagner USA

Acceptable stereotypes?

Many of the cartoons in this section are quite clear stereotype images, or make a play on stereotypes. Cartoons of this type can be used to stimulate a discussion on the nature of stereotyping and the role that we ourselves have to play in it.

Ask individuals to have a quick look at each of the cartoons and to identify [on the basis of this initial viewing] those they like most and those they do not like. Then discuss their choices with a partner and see whether they choose similar ones.

• What do they think the cartoonists were attempting to say in those they did not like?

• Was, for example, the cartoonist attempting to use the stereotype to reinforce the idea or to encourage questioning?

• Do we have different ideas about the intentions of the cartoonist, what does this imply?

A discussion of this nature could be usefully followed up by considering the context in which cartoons are used. Would that make any difference to the implications of the stereotype? It may also be useful to review the notion that we all have stereotypes and use them .

• What are our acceptable stereotypes?

• Can we become more aware of them and how they influence our thinking?

• Do we all have similar ones? Should we have?

White is wearing rings in your ears while laughing at people who wear rings in their noses.

THE ELECTION POSTER.

Fuchsel Denmark

"Goodness me! We don't all run about in silk shirts and Italian suits, you know."

Donegan

122

The Russians

"Ask them how many beads for a full service and a new half-shaft."

Dickinson   Britain

God! How divinely Third World!

Steve Bell   Britain

R. Cobb   Australia

It's only some foreign aid mission members, sir. I told them we wanted to be self-reliant and didn't want to depend on any country and sent them away!

Laxman   India

M.   Australia

"I still can't tell 'em apart."

Alan Dunn   USA

'And to ensure a balanced and impartial discussion of the latest government measures I have with me a government spokesman and a wild-eyed Trot from the lunatic fringe'.

Lowry   Britain

Cummings

ARAB WORLD Unspeakable!

COMMUNIST BLOCK Ghastly!

E.E.C. Maddening.

S. AMERICA Hopeless.

BLACK AFRICA Dreadful!

CHINA

VIENNA CONVENTION
Please use the correct knife & fork, and do not blow on your soup.

"I wish I could break off diplomatic relations with ALL foreigners"

Cummings   Britain

AND I'M TELLING YOU THE PRESIDENT IS EXPECTING ME... SOMETHING ABOUT A POSITION IN HUMAN RIGHTS...

Auth   USA

OUR POLICEMEN ARE WONDERFUL.

Evans   Britain

Malcolm Hancock USA

"WHEN I GROW UP – I'M GONNA BE WHITE.."

R. Cobb   Australia

Cummings

"I wish I had taken the Pill!"

BRITANNIA – 'MOTHER' OF THE COMMONWEALTH – AND HER CHILDREN

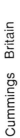

Cummings   Britain

"If you want to know who we are,
We are gentlemen of Japan."

Rea Irvin   USA

Christian USA

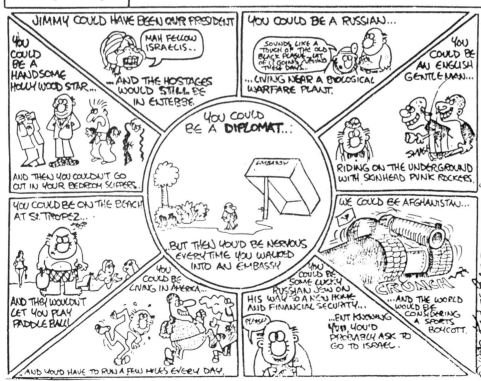

Kirscher South Africa

To read

75.25 Ireland in an unequal world
[Colm Regan et al, CONGOOD, 1984.]
A comprehensive introduction to development issues. Links made with local issues in Ireland. Also useful as reference book.

Nothing but the same old story
The roots of anti-Irish racism.
[Liz Curtis Information on Ireland., 1984]
A fully illustrated historical analysis of British attitudes and images of the Irish.

Half the lies are True - Britain/Ireland a microcosm of international misunderstanding [Colm Regan and Scott Sinclair (Ed), Trocaire/DEC ,1986 .]
(see back page)

Dressed to kill - Cartoonists and the Northern Ireland Conflict
[John Darby, Appletree Press, 1983.]
A useful collection of cartoons. A very full analysis of the role of cartoons, cartoonists and a valuable resource on Northern Ireland.

Hidden Messages - activities for exploring bias
[Catherine McFarlane et al (DEC Birmingham) 1986.]
Practical classroom activities for building up skills in awareness of the nature of bias.

Comics and Magazines
[J. Hemmings and J. Leggett ILEA English Centre, 1984.]
Stimulus for students to analyse the messages of teenage comics and magazines.

Plugs

Martyn Turner's Books In Print
(The first one sold out, eventually)

'Illuminations,
101 Drawings from Early Irish History'

This was published late in 1986 by the Boethius Press, Kilkenny. It is an attempt to treat old myths and legends the same way new myths and legends are treated in the pages of the Irish Times. There are 10 full colour drawings, A4 sideways, hardback at the exorbitant price of £11.95 (£11.50 sterling) from Boethius Press, Clarabricken, Co.Kilkenny.

'A Fistful of Dailers'

This was published by Gill and MacMillan in 1987. It is chock full of political cartoons from 1983 to 1987 and costs the exorbitant price of £6.95 Irish....... wait'til its remaindered.

These cartoons are all saying something about "dialogue" and change. What do they suggest? Is this a fair representation of the political processes of change? There are many other cartoons in this book which could be used to raise questions about the nature of such dialogue.